Southern Living.

Easy
Weeknight
Favorites

Southern Living.

OUR BEST

Easy
Weeknight
Favorites

Compiled by
Jean Wickstrom Liles

Edited by
Julie Fisher

OXMOOR
HOUSE.

© 1998 by Oxmoor House, Inc.
Book Division of Southern Progress Corporation
P.O. Box 2463, Birmingham, Alabama 35201

Southern Living® is a federally registered trademark of Southern Living, Inc.

Library of Congress Catalog Card Number: 97-69946
ISBN: 0-8487-1686-8
Manufactured in the United States of America
Twelfth Printing 2004

To order additional publications, call 1-800-765-6400.

For more books to enrich your life, visit
oxmoorhouse.com

Editor-in-Chief: Nancy Fitzpatrick Wyatt
Senior Foods Editor: Susan Carlisle Payne
Senior Editor, Editorial Services: Olivia Kindig Wells
Art Director: James Boone

Southern Living® *Our Best Easy Weeknight Favorites*
Editor: Julie Fisher
Copy Editor: Keri Bradford Anderson
Associate Art Director: Cynthia R. Cooper
Senior Designer: Melissa Jones Clark
Designer: Clare T. Minges
Editorial Assistant: Catherine S. Ritter
Director, Test Kitchens: Kathleen Royal Phillips
Assistant Director, Test Kitchens: Gayle Hays Sadler
Test Kitchens Staff: Molly Baldwin, Susan Hall Bellows,
    Julie Christopher, Natalie E. King, Elizabeth Tyler Luckett,
    Jan Jacks Moon, Iris Crawley O'Brien, Jan A. Smith
Menu and Recipe Consultant: Jean Wickstrom Liles
Senior Photographer: Jim Bathie
Photographers: Brit Huckabay, John O'Hagan
Senior Photo Stylist: Kay E. Clarke
Photo Stylist: Virginia R. Cravens
Publishing Systems Administrator: Rick Tucker
Production Director: Phillip Lee
Associate Production Manager: Theresa L. Beste
Production Assistant: Faye Porter Bonner

Cover: *Tortilla Pie* (page 106)
Back Cover: *Nacho Chicken* (page 80)
Page 2: *Simple Tiramisù* (page 21)

We Want Your FAVORITE RECIPES!

Southern Living cooks are simply the best cooks, and we want your secrets! Please send your favorite original recipes and a sentence about why you like each one. We can't guarantee we'll print them in a cookbook, but if we do, we'll send you $10 and a free copy of the cookbook. Send each recipe on a separate page, with your name, address, and daytime phone number to:

Cookbook Recipes
Oxmoor House
2100 Lakeshore Drive
Birmingham, AL 35209

Contents

A Weeknight Welcome

If a fast-paced lifestyle leaves you little time for cooking, *Our Best Easy Weeknight Favorites* was created for you. It's your key to hassle-free dinners night after night. These family-filling recipes and menus will help you cook with confidence and speed—so you can enjoy great taste with little effort.

Browse through the pages and look for these features designed to let you have dinner on the table in minutes, even on the busiest nights.

- **More than 300 superquick-and-easy recipes fill these pages.**
- **Each recipe gives you preparation and cook times.**
- **Short ingredient lists abound.** You'll find innovative ways to use high-quality convenience products and readily available ingredients.
- **You'll need few utensils and pieces of cooking equipment.** Our shortcut cooking directions simplify meal preparation and cleanup.
- **A month of quick-fix weeknight menus awaits.** And each menu goes from pantry to table in less than an hour. All have photographs, and many include a grocery list, equipment list, and foolproof menu plan.
- **Variations and substitutions are here for you.** Follow tips to adapt recipes to what's on hand in your kitchen.
- **Fifty Timeshavers** will keep fun in your cooking. Turn the page to see these clever shortcuts.

PAGE 80

PAGE 179

PAGE 113

PAGE 228

PAGE 84

50 Timeshavers

These quick tips will get you in and out of the kitchen in no time.

STOCKING AND SHOPPING:

1. Keep your pantry and freezer well stocked with basic ingredients that you commonly use for quick and easy cooking.

2. Shop at a full-service supermarket. It will have the largest selection of convenience products.

3. Write your grocery shopping list in categories that match the aisles in the store, such as dairy, produce, baking needs, and frozen items. Learn the layout of your grocery store, and you'll be surprised how fast you can shop.

4. Keep an ongoing grocery list posted on the refrigerator, and jot down items as soon as they begin to run low.

EQUIPMENT:

5. Place a canister or utensil jar next to the cooktop, and keep your favorite tools—wooden spoons, spatulas, potato masher, meat fork, and whisk—within easy reach.

6. Use a mini or regular food processor to chop green peppers, onions, and herbs. Designate a coffee grinder for grinding whole spices. (Be sure to clean it well between uses.)

7. Use your microwave often. It's great for baking potatoes, cooking vegetables, boiling water, toasting nuts, warming tortillas, cooking bacon, and melting chocolate or butter.

8. Invest in a gas grill. It heats up instantly, and cleanup is simple.

9. Cover your grill to cook foods faster and to enhance the smoky flavor.

10. Use kitchen shears to trim fat from raw meat, snip fresh herbs, chop dried fruit, cut up mini pizzas or pita bread, and chop canned tomatoes right in the can.

11. Collect nonstick cookware and bakeware.

12. Use a coarse grater to grate a cold stick of butter when a pie or casserole needs a dot of butter.

13. Use a swivel-bladed vegetable peeler when you need a little grated cheese to top a burger or garnish a salad. Or use it to shave chocolate curls from a square of chocolate to decorate a cake.

14. Use a pizza cutter to make quick cuts in dough or pastry; or use it to cut French bread for croutons.

15. Freeze single servings of soup, chili, or spaghetti sauce in individual microwave-safe containers. Or use heavy-duty, zip-top freezer bags, which stack easily and don't take up much space.

16. Use an egg slicer to slice whole strawberries and mushrooms, hard-cooked eggs, firm bananas, and peeled kiwifruit.

17. Use a fork, potato masher, or pastry blender to mash bananas, squash, or sweet potatoes for casseroles or breads.

INGREDIENTS:

18. Buy minced garlic in a jar (look for it in the produce section of the grocery store).

19. Chop extra green pepper or onion and freeze it in zip-top freezer bags for later use.

20. Buy roasted red peppers in a jar instead of roasting your own.

21. Purchase bags of trimmed and cleaned mixed greens for easy salads.

22. Have your grocer peel, devein, and steam shrimp for you. Call in your order ahead of time.

23. Use dried herbs, and keep them in the freezer, arranged alphabetically, for optimal flavor and easy access.

24. Use canned beans instead of dried ones. No soaking's needed, and you can use them on a moment's notice.

25. Buy canned ready-to-serve broth instead of making it.

26. Purchase cheese that's already shredded.

27. Buy chicken breast tenders, so you don't have to spend the time cutting up chicken (especially for stir-fry).

28. Purchase deli-roasted chicken; then shred or chop it to use in recipes calling for cooked chicken.

29. Buy frozen chopped vegetables. Many recipes use them straight from the freezer—no thawing needed.

30. Choose boil-in-bag rice. It's the faithful 10-minute rice, available in several flavors.

31. Bake commercial cheese pizza crusts (like Boboli) in a mere 6 to 8 minutes. Their versatility goes beyond pizza.

32. Keep a bottle of zesty Italian dressing on hand. It's a great marinade for meats, chicken, seafood, vegetable kabobs, or antipasto platters.

33. Keep a carton of frozen whipped topping in the freezer. It can garnish almost any dessert.

PROCEDURES:
34. Toast nuts in a dry skillet over medium heat. Shake the skillet until you begin to smell the nuts toasting.

35. Place a metal colander upside down over a skillet when browning meat or frying bacon to prevent splatters.

36. Chill glasses in the freezer for frosty beverages in a hurry.

37. Marinate ingredients in heavy-duty, zip-top plastic bags. You'll have no bowls to clean.

38. Use a leafy stalk of celery instead of a basting brush to baste foods. This will eliminate brush washing and will add extra flavor to the food you're grilling.

39. Puree fresh berries or peaches in a blender with an equal amount of cream, and serve the mixture as a dessert sauce over pound cake or ice cream.

40. Freeze extra tomato sauce, gravy, or broth in ice cube trays; then reheat cubes as needed in soups and main-dish recipes.

41. Speed the ripening of a green banana by heating it, unpeeled, at 350° for 5 minutes.

42. Brown a pound of ground beef and a chopped onion. Pack it in 1-cup freezer containers. When you need a quick meal, thaw a portion for tacos, sloppy joes, or spaghetti.

43. Freeze your favorite cookie dough in a log wrapped in wax paper. Then slice from the frozen log, and bake as needed, a few slices at a time.

44. Save the butter wrapper in the refrigerator after you've used a stick of butter. Use it to grease a cookie sheet or loafpan the next time you bake.

CLEANUP:
45. Line your broiler pan with aluminum foil for instant cleanup.

46. Use a spray-on oven cleaner on really dirty pots and pans to ease cleanup.

47. Soak dirty dishes in hot, soapy water as you're preparing a meal, and you won't have to scrub them as much later.

48. Use disposable foil pans when you won't have time to clean up.

49. Spray measuring cups and spoons with vegetable cooking spray before measuring honey or molasses. The sticky liquids will slide right out.

50. Spray a grater with cooking spray before shredding soft cheese. The grater will be easier to clean.

PAGE 28

PAGE 30

PAGE 12

PAGE 24

PAGE 16

PAGE 14

Menus At

Quick Menus

Begin on page 12

TEN MOUTHWATERING MENUS PROMISE DINNER IN 45 MINUTES—START TO FINISH. WE PROVIDE THE MAIN-DISH RECIPE PLUS ONE ACCOMPANIMENT, AND THEN GIVE IDEAS FOR CONVENIENCE PRODUCTS TO FILL YOUR PLATE.

PAGE 37

PAGE 40

A Glance

PAGE 41

PAGE 42

Superquick Menus

Begin on page 32

IF YOU'RE REALLY IN A HURRY, TRY ONE OF THESE SPEEDY SUPPERS. EACH YIELDS A DELICIOUS MEAL IN 30 MINUTES. WE GIVE YOU THE ENTRÉE RECIPE AND SUGGEST A "NO-RECIPE-NEEDED" SIDE DISH, BREAD, AND DESSERT.

PAGE 34

PAGE 33

A Taste of Tex-Mex

Weeknight Enchiladas

Refried Beans

Shredded Lettuce with Guacamole

Toffee Surprise

Serves 4

Weeknight Enchiladas

PREP: 7 MINUTES   COOK: 29 MINUTES

1 pound ground chuck
1 small onion, chopped
1 (10¾-ounce) can tomato
    soup, undiluted
1 (10-ounce) can mild
    enchilada sauce

8 (7- or 8-inch) flour tortillas
2 cups (8 ounces) shredded
    Cheddar cheese, divided
Sour cream (optional)
Sliced ripe olives (optional)

Cook beef and onion in a large skillet over medium-high heat until meat is browned, stirring until it crumbles; drain and return to skillet.

   Stir soup and enchilada sauce into meat mixture. Spread ¼ cup meat mixture onto each tortilla; sprinkle tortillas evenly with 1 cup cheese. Roll up tortillas; place, seam side down, in a greased 13- x 9- x 2-inch baking dish. Pour remaining meat mixture over tortillas.

   Cover and bake at 350° for 20 minutes. Uncover and sprinkle with remaining 1 cup cheese; bake 5 more minutes or until cheese melts. Serve with sour cream and olives, if desired. Yield: 4 servings.

Toffee Surprise

PREP: 9 MINUTES

1 quart vanilla ice cream
4 (1¼-ounce) English
    toffee-flavored candy bars,
    coarsely crushed

¼ cup Kahlúa or other
    coffee-flavored liqueur

Spoon ice cream and crushed toffee bars evenly into four parfait glasses or dessert dishes. Just before serving, top each with 1 tablespoon Kahlúa. Yield: 4 servings.

GROCERIES NEEDED

- 1 pound ground chuck
- 1 small onion
- 1 (10¾-ounce) can
   tomato soup
- 1 (10-ounce) can mild
   enchilada sauce
- Package flour tortillas
- 8 ounces Cheddar cheese
- Sour cream
- Can sliced ripe olives
- 1 quart vanilla ice cream
- 4 (1¼-ounce) English
   toffee candy bars
- ¼ cup Kahlúa (from
   liquor store)
- 1 (16-ounce) can refried
   beans
- 1 (4.5-ounce) can
   chopped green chiles
- Lettuce
- Commercial guacamole

EQUIPMENT NEEDED

- Large skillet
- 13- x 9- x 2-inch baking
   dish
- Saucepan

MENU PLAN

1. Prepare Toffee Surprise, but don't add Kahlúa; freeze until serving time.

2. Prepare enchiladas.

3. While enchiladas bake, shred lettuce, and heat refried beans with green chiles in a saucepan over low heat.

4. Sprinkle cheese on enchiladas; bake 5 more minutes.

5. Top each dessert with Kahlúa just before serving.

Sunset Supper

Herbed Shrimp and Pasta

Sliced Tomatoes

Dilled Garlic Bread

Pound Cake

Serves 6

Herbed Shrimp and Pasta

PREP: 5 MINUTES   COOK: 20 MINUTES

8 ounces dried angel hair
   pasta, uncooked
1 cup butter
1½ pounds peeled, medium-
   size fresh shrimp
   (2 pounds unpeeled)
4 cloves garlic, minced
2 cups half-and-half

½ cup chopped fresh parsley
½ teaspoon salt
¼ teaspoon pepper
2 teaspoons chopped fresh
   dillweed or ¾ teaspoon
   dried dillweed (optional)
Garnish: fresh dillweed sprigs

Cook pasta according to package directions. Drain; set aside, and keep warm.

  Meanwhile, melt butter in a large heavy skillet over medium-high heat; add shrimp and garlic. Cook, stirring constantly, 3 to 5 minutes or until shrimp turn pink. Remove shrimp, and set aside, reserving garlic and butter in skillet.

  Add half-and-half to skillet; bring to a boil, stirring gently. Reduce heat, and simmer 15 minutes or until thickened, stirring occasionally. Add shrimp, parsley, salt, pepper, and, if desired, chopped dillweed; stir until blended. Serve over pasta. Garnish, if desired. Yield: 6 servings.

Dilled Garlic Bread

PREP: 10 MINUTES   COOK: 10 MINUTES

⅓ cup butter or margarine,
   softened
¼ cup finely chopped fresh
   dillweed
2 large cloves garlic, crushed

1 (16-ounce) loaf unsliced
   French bread
¼ cup grated Parmesan
   cheese

Combine first 3 ingredients. Slice loaf in half lengthwise. Spread butter mixture evenly on cut sides of bread. Sprinkle with cheese. Place on an ungreased baking sheet. Bake at 375° for 10 minutes or until browned. Slice and serve hot. Yield: 1 loaf.

GROCERIES NEEDED

Check staples: butter or margarine, salt, pepper
- 8 ounces dried angel hair pasta
- 1½ pounds peeled, medium-size fresh shrimp
- Fresh garlic
- 2 cups half-and-half
- Bunch fresh parsley
- Bunch fresh dillweed
- 1 (16-ounce) loaf unsliced French bread
- ¼ cup grated Parmesan cheese
- Fresh tomatoes
- Pound cake

EQUIPMENT NEEDED
- Dutch oven
- Colander
- Large heavy skillet
- Baking sheet

MENU PLAN

1. Soften butter for bread.

2. Cook pasta; keep warm.

3. While pasta cooks, prepare shrimp cream sauce.

4. Prepare and bake garlic bread.

5. Slice tomatoes and pound cake just before serving.

Casual Night

Three-Pepper Pork Cutlets

Rice Pilaf with Vegetables

Fried Apples

Broccoli Spears

Cinnamon Ice Cream

Serves 4

Three-Pepper Pork Cutlets

PREP: 10 MINUTES   COOK: 8 MINUTES

1 (1-pound) pork tenderloin	¼ teaspoon black pepper
1 teaspoon paprika	⅛ teaspoon ground red
1 teaspoon dried thyme	pepper
½ teaspoon dried oregano	1 teaspoon olive oil
½ teaspoon dried rosemary,	2 cloves garlic, crushed
crushed	Vegetable cooking spray
¼ teaspoon salt	
¼ teaspoon ground white	
pepper	

Cut pork crosswise into 12 slices. Place each pork slice between two sheets of heavy-duty plastic wrap, and flatten to ¼-inch thickness, using the heel of your hand or a meat mallet.

Combine paprika and next 9 ingredients; rub over both sides of pork slices. Place pork on a broiler rack coated with cooking spray; place rack in a broiler pan. Broil 5½ inches from heat (with electric oven door partially opened) 3 to 4 minutes on each side or until done. Yield: 4 servings.

Cinnamon Ice Cream

PREP: 10 MINUTES

1 quart vanilla ice cream,	1 teaspoon ground cinnamon
slightly softened	Hot fudge topping

Stir together ice cream and cinnamon in a large bowl. Refreeze, if desired. Scoop into serving dishes, and drizzle with fudge topping. Yield: 4 servings.

GROCERIES NEEDED

Check staples: paprika, dried thyme, dried oregano, dried rosemary, salt, ground white pepper, black pepper, ground red pepper, olive oil, vegetable cooking spray, ground cinnamon

- 1 pound pork tenderloin
- Fresh garlic
- 1 (16-ounce) bag frozen rice pilaf with vegetables
- 1 (28-ounce) jar fried apples
- 1 (16-ounce) package frozen broccoli spears
- 1 quart vanilla ice cream
- Hot fudge topping

EQUIPMENT NEEDED

- Meat mallet
- Broiler pan with rack
- Saucepan with lid

MENU PLAN

1. Soften ice cream, and stir in cinnamon; freeze until serving time.

2. Cook rice pilaf and broccoli according to package directions; keep warm.

3. While side dishes cook, prepare pork.

4. Heat apples in a saucepan, if desired.

5. Scoop ice cream into serving dishes, and top with fudge sauce before serving.

Family-Pleasing Chicken

Creamy Chicken Casserole

Green Beans

Mandarin Orange and Lettuce Salad

Apple Pie

Serves 4

Creamy Chicken Casserole

PREP: 5 MINUTES   COOK: 30 MINUTES

3 cups chopped cooked
    chicken
1 (10¾-ounce) can cream of
    chicken soup, undiluted
1 (8-ounce) carton sour cream
1 tablespoon poppy seeds

1½ cups crushed round
     buttery crackers (40
     crackers)
¼ cup butter or margarine,
    melted

Combine first 4 ingredients; spoon into a lightly greased 11- x 7- x 1½-inch baking dish. Combine crushed crackers and butter, and sprinkle over chicken mixture. Bake, uncovered, at 350° for 30 minutes. Yield: 4 servings.

Mandarin Orange and Lettuce Salad

PREP: 5 MINUTES

6 cups torn mixed greens or 1
    (16-ounce) package mixed
    lettuces
1 (11-ounce) can mandarin
    oranges, drained
⅓ cup golden raisins

1 (2-ounce) package cashew
    nuts, toasted (⅓ cup)
½ cup commercial Italian
    salad dressing or sweet-
    and-sour salad dressing

Combine first 4 ingredients in a salad bowl. Pour salad dressing over salad, and toss. Serve immediately. Yield: 4 servings.

GROCERIES NEEDED

Check staples: poppy seeds, butter or margarine
- 3 cups chopped cooked chicken
- 1 (10¾-ounce) can cream of chicken soup
- 1 (8-ounce) carton sour cream
- Round buttery crackers
- 6 cups torn mixed greens or 1 (16-ounce) package mixed lettuces
- 1 (11-ounce) can mandarin oranges
- ⅓ cup golden raisins
- 1 (2-ounce) package cashew nuts (⅓ cup)
- Commercial Italian or sweet-and-sour salad dressing
- 1½ pounds fresh or frozen green beans
- Commercial apple pie

EQUIPMENT NEEDED
- 11- x 7- x 1½-inch baking dish
- Saucepan

MENU PLAN

1. Prepare and bake chicken casserole.

2. While casserole bakes, trim and cook green beans, and toast cashews for salad.

3. Prepare salad.

4. Heat pie during dinner.

Italian Fare

Quick Carbonara
Green Salad
Crusty Rolls
Simple Tiramisù

Serves 4

Quick Carbonara

PREP: 10 MINUTES   COOK: 19 MINUTES

1 (8-ounce) package spaghetti,
  uncooked
8 slices bacon
⅔ cup chopped green onions
1 (4-ounce) can sliced
  mushrooms, drained
3 egg yolks, lightly beaten
1 to 1½ cups (4 to 6 ounces)
  finely shredded Cheddar
  cheese
Dash of pepper

Cook pasta according to package directions. Meanwhile, cook bacon in a large skillet until crisp; remove bacon, reserving 3 tablespoons drippings in skillet. Coarsely crumble bacon, and set aside.

Cook green onions and mushrooms in drippings in skillet over medium heat 2 minutes. Drain pasta, and place in a serving bowl. Stir egg yolks into hot pasta immediately after draining it. Stir in bacon, green onions and mushrooms, cheese, and pepper; toss. Serve immediately. Yield: 4 servings.

Simple Tiramisù

PREP: 15 MINUTES   FREEZE: 30 MINUTES

1 (8-ounce) package cream
  cheese, softened
¾ cup strongly brewed
  coffee, cooled
3 (1-ounce) squares semisweet
  chocolate, grated
¾ cup chopped almonds,
  toasted and divided
1 (12-ounce) container frozen
  whipped topping, thawed
2 (3-ounce) packages
  ladyfingers, split
Garnish: additional grated
  semisweet chocolate

Beat cream cheese in a large mixing bowl at high speed of an electric mixer until light and fluffy. Add ¼ cup coffee, beating just until blended. Stir in 3 squares grated chocolate and ½ cup almonds. Set aside 1 cup whipped topping. Fold remaining whipped topping into cream cheese mixture.

Brush cut sides of ladyfingers thoroughly with remaining ½ cup coffee. Arrange two-thirds of ladyfingers on bottom and up sides of a 2-quart bowl (such as a large mixing bowl); spoon cream cheese mixture into center. Top with remaining ladyfingers and reserved 1 cup whipped topping; sprinkle with remaining ¼ cup almonds. Cover and freeze 30 minutes. Garnish, if desired. Yield: 8 servings.

GROCERIES NEEDED

Check staples: 3 egg yolks, pepper
- 1 (8-ounce) package spaghetti
- 8 slices bacon
- Bunch green onions
- 1 (4-ounce) can sliced mushrooms
- 4 to 6 ounces Cheddar cheese
- 1 (8-ounce) package cream cheese
- Coffee
- 3 to 4 (1-ounce) squares semisweet chocolate
- ¾ cup chopped almonds
- 1 (12-ounce) container frozen whipped topping
- 2 (3-ounce) packages ladyfingers
- Makings for green salad
- Crusty rolls

EQUIPMENT NEEDED
- Dutch oven
- Colander
- Large skillet
- Electric mixer
- Pastry brush

MENU PLAN

1. Prepare tiramisù; freeze until serving time.

2. Cook pasta.

3. While pasta cooks, toss salad ingredients, and finish preparing carbonara.

4. Heat rolls, if desired.

Patio Supper

Sausage-Stuffed French Loaf

Cucumber-Tomato Salad

Potato Chips

Chocolate Chip Cookies

Serves 4

Sausage-Stuffed French Loaf

PREP: 11 MINUTES   **COOK: 29 MINUTES**

1 (16-ounce) loaf unsliced French bread
½ pound ground pork sausage
½ pound ground chuck
1 medium onion, chopped
1 cup (4 ounces) shredded mozzarella cheese
1 large egg, lightly beaten

¼ cup chopped fresh parsley
1 teaspoon Dijon mustard
¼ teaspoon fennel seeds
¼ teaspoon salt
¼ teaspoon pepper
2 tablespoons butter or margarine
1 large clove garlic, crushed

Cut off ends of loaf; set ends aside. Hollow out center of loaf with a long serrated bread knife, leaving a ½-inch shell. Position knife blade in food processor bowl; add bread removed from inside loaf. Process to make coarse crumbs. Set bread shell and crumbs aside.

Cook sausage, beef, and onion in a large skillet over medium-high heat until meat is browned, stirring until it crumbles; drain. Add 1 cup of reserved breadcrumbs, cheese, and next 6 ingredients; stir well. Spoon meat mixture into shell; replace loaf ends, securing with wooden picks.

Melt butter in a saucepan. Add garlic; cook about 1 minute. Brush butter mixture over loaf. Wrap loaf in aluminum foil, leaving open slightly on top; place loaf on a baking sheet. Bake at 400° for 25 minutes or until loaf is heated and cheese melts. Cut into 4 pieces. Yield: 4 servings.

Cucumber-Tomato Salad

PREP: 8 MINUTES

3 tablespoons olive oil
1½ tablespoons lemon juice
1 teaspoon Dijon mustard
⅛ teaspoon salt
⅛ teaspoon pepper
⅓ cup sliced ripe olives, drained

2 tomatoes, cut into 8 wedges each
1 medium cucumber, sliced
Lettuce leaves

Combine first 5 ingredients, stirring well with a fork or small whisk. Combine olives, tomato, and cucumber in a bowl. Pour dressing mixture over tomato mixture; toss. Cover and chill 30 minutes, if desired. Serve on lettuce leaves. Yield: 4 servings.

GROCERIES NEEDED

Check staples: egg, Dijon mustard, fennel seeds, salt, pepper, butter or margarine, olive oil
- 1 (16-ounce) loaf unsliced French bread
- ½ pound ground pork sausage
- ½ pound ground chuck
- 1 medium onion
- 4 ounces mozzarella cheese
- Bunch fresh parsley
- Fresh garlic
- 1½ tablespoons lemon juice
- ⅓ cup sliced ripe olives
- 2 tomatoes
- 1 medium cucumber
- Lettuce leaves
- Potato chips
- Refrigerated chocolate chip cookie dough

EQUIPMENT NEEDED

- Serrated bread knife
- Food processor (optional)
- Large skillet
- Small saucepan
- Pastry brush
- Baking sheet

MENU PLAN

1. Prepare and bake stuffed sausage loaf.

2. While loaf bakes, prepare salad; cover and chill.

3. Bake cookies according to package directions.

Splurge Supper

Filet Mignon with Horseradish Gravy
Mashed Potatoes Steamed Asparagus
Greek Salad French Bread
Commercial Cheesecake

Serves 4

Filet Mignon with Horseradish Gravy

PREP: 2 MINUTES   COOK: 20 MINUTES

4 (5-ounce) beef tenderloin
     steaks
¼ teaspoon salt
¼ teaspoon pepper
1 (¾-ounce) package brown
     gravy mix

½ cup water
½ cup red wine
2½ tablespoons prepared
     horseradish
1 (8-ounce) package sliced
     fresh mushrooms

Heat a heavy nonstick skillet over medium-high heat until hot. Sprinkle steaks with salt and pepper. Add steaks to hot skillet; cook 1 minute on each side. Place steaks in a greased small baking dish.

  Add gravy mix and next 3 ingredients to skillet. Bring to a boil; reduce heat, and simmer, stirring constantly, until thickened. Stir in mushrooms. Pour mixture over steaks. Bake, uncovered, at 350° for 15 minutes or to desired doneness. Yield: 4 servings.

Greek Salad

PREP: 14 MINUTES

1 medium head iceberg
     lettuce, torn
1 small purple onion, thinly
     sliced
½ cup pepperoncini salad
     peppers

½ cup kalamata olives
4 ounces crumbled feta cheese
½ cup commercial red wine
     vinaigrette

Combine all ingredients in a salad bowl; toss gently. Serve immediately. Yield: 4 servings.

Check staples: salt, pepper, prepared horseradish
- 4 (5-ounce) beef tenderloin steaks
- 1 (¾-ounce) package brown gravy mix
- Red wine
- 1 (8-ounce) package sliced fresh mushrooms
- 1 medium head iceberg lettuce
- 1 small purple onion
- ½ cup pepperoncini salad peppers
- ½ cup kalamata olives
- 4 ounces feta cheese
- Commercial red wine vinaigrette
- 4 baking potatoes or 1 box of instant mashed potatoes
- 1 pound fresh asparagus
- French bread
- Commercial frozen cheesecake

EQUIPMENT NEEDED

- Heavy nonstick skillet
- Small baking dish
- Asparagus steamer

MENU PLAN

1. Prepare filet mignon.

2. Microwave potatoes; then mash them. (Or prepare instant mashed potatoes according to package directions.)

3. While steaks cook, trim and steam asparagus.

4. Toss salad at the last minute.

Before the Game

Speedy Chili Dogs

Easy Coleslaw

Potato Chips

Brownies

Serves 8

Speedy Chili Dogs

PREP: 5 MINUTES   **COOK: 35 MINUTES**

1 pound ground chuck
1 large onion, chopped (2 cups)
1 clove garlic, crushed
1 (15-ounce) can tomato sauce
2 tablespoons chili powder
¼ teaspoon salt
⅛ teaspoon pepper
1 cup water
8 frankfurters, cooked
8 hot dog buns, split and toasted
2 cups (8 ounces) shredded mild Cheddar cheese
Chopped green onions

Combine first 3 ingredients in a large skillet, and cook over medium-high heat until beef is browned, stirring until it crumbles; drain. Add tomato sauce and next 4 ingredients. Bring to a boil; cover, reduce heat, and simmer 25 minutes, stirring occasionally.

Place frankfurters in buns. Spoon chili mixture over frankfurters; top with cheese and green onions. Yield: 8 servings.

Easy Coleslaw

PREP: 2 MINUTES

1 (16-ounce) package coleslaw*
1 (8-ounce) bottle coleslaw dressing*
¼ teaspoon salt
¼ teaspoon pepper

Combine all ingredients in a large bowl, tossing well. Serve immediately, or cover and chill. Yield: 6 cups.

*For coleslaw, we used River Ranch. For coleslaw dressing, we used Kraft.

GROCERIES NEEDED

Check staples: chili powder, salt, pepper
- 1 pound ground chuck
- 1 large onion
- Fresh garlic
- 1 (15-ounce) can tomato sauce
- 8 frankfurters
- 8 hot dog buns
- 8 ounces mild Cheddar cheese
- Bunch green onions
- Potato chips
- 1 (16-ounce) package coleslaw
- 1 (8-ounce) bottle coleslaw dressing
- Brownies

EQUIPMENT NEEDED
- Large skillet with lid
- Large saucepan

MENU PLAN

1. Cook ground beef mixture for chili dogs.

2. While beef mixture simmers, cook frankfurters.

3. Prepare coleslaw. Chill, if desired.

4. Split and toast buns; assemble chili dogs.

Faux-Fried Favorites

Oven-Fried Fish

Zesty French Fries

Turnip Greens   Corn on the Cob

Lemon Frappé

Serves 4

Oven-Fried Fish

PREP: 5 MINUTES   **COOK: 10 MINUTES**

¼ cup white cornmeal
¼ cup fine, dry breadcrumbs
½ teaspoon salt
½ teaspoon paprika
1½ teaspoons chopped fresh
  dillweed or ½ teaspoon
  dried dillweed
⅛ teaspoon pepper

1 pound fresh or frozen fish
  fillets, thawed
⅓ cup milk
3 tablespoons butter or
  margarine, melted
Lemon wedges
Tartar sauce

Combine first 6 ingredients in a shallow dish. Dip fish fillets in milk, and dredge in cornmeal mixture. Place coated fish in a lightly greased 13- x 9- x 2-inch pan; drizzle with butter.

Bake at 450° for 10 minutes or until fish flakes easily when tested with a fork. Serve with lemon wedges and tartar sauce. Yield: 4 servings.

Lemon Frappé

PREP: 4 MINUTES

1 (6-ounce) can frozen
  lemonade concentrate,
  undiluted
½ cup cold water

1 pint lemon sherbet or
  vanilla ice cream*
1 (12-ounce) can ginger ale

Combine first 3 ingredients in container of an electric blender; cover and process until smooth, stopping once to scrape down sides. Pour into a serving pitcher; add ginger ale. Serve immediately. Yield: 4 cups.

*Plenty of lemon flavor prevails if you use vanilla ice cream in this slushy dessert beverage. To make **Lime Frappés,** use a 6-ounce can limeade in place of lemonade concentrate.

GROCERIES NEEDED

Check staples: cornmeal, salt, paprika, pepper, milk, butter or margarine
- Fine, dry breadcrumbs
- Fresh or dried dillweed
- 1 pound fresh or frozen fish fillets
- 1 or 2 lemons
- Tartar sauce
- 1 (32-ounce) bag frozen French fries (we used Ore-Ida Zesties)
- 1 (10- or 16-ounce) package frozen turnip greens
- 4 ears of corn or 1 (16-ounce) package frozen corn
- 1 (6-ounce) can frozen lemonade concentrate
- 1 pint lemon sherbet or vanilla ice cream
- 1 (12-ounce) can ginger ale

EQUIPMENT NEEDED
- Shallow dish
- 13- x 9- x 2-inch pan
- Electric blender
- Baking sheet

MENU PLAN

1. Bake fries according to package directions. Bring water to a boil for corn, if cooking fresh ears.

2. Microwave turnip greens according to package directions; boil fresh corn, or cook frozen corn according to package directions.

3. While fries bake, prepare fish. Add fish to bake in oven during last 10 minutes fries bake.

4. Blend frappés after dinner.

Soup and Sandwich Night

Cream of Pimiento Soup

Grilled Ham and Cheese

Serves 4

Cream of Pimiento Soup

PREP: 2 MINUTES   COOK: 20 MINUTES

1 (4-ounce) jar diced
  pimiento, undrained
3 tablespoons butter or
  margarine
3 tablespoons all-purpose
  flour
1 (14½-ounce) can ready-to-
  serve chicken broth

1½ cups half-and-half
2 teaspoons grated onion
½ teaspoon salt
¼ teaspoon hot sauce
Garnish: sour cream

Place pimiento in container of an electric blender; cover and process until smooth, stopping once to scrape down sides. Set aside.

Melt butter in a heavy saucepan over low heat; add flour, stirring until smooth. Cook, stirring constantly, 1 minute. Gradually add broth and half-and-half to saucepan; cook over medium heat, stirring constantly, until thickened and bubbly.

Stir in pimiento, onion, salt, and hot sauce; cook over medium-low heat, stirring constantly, until heated. Garnish, if desired. Yield: 3½ cups.

Grilled Ham and Cheese

PREP: 8 MINUTES   COOK: 4 MINUTES

1 cup (4 ounces) shredded
  Monterey Jack cheese
1 cup (4 ounces) shredded
  Cheddar cheese
¼ cup mayonnaise
1 tablespoon prepared
  mustard

1 green onion, finely chopped
8 slices sandwich bread
4 slices sandwich ham
¼ cup butter or margarine,
  softened

Combine first 5 ingredients. Spread cheese mixture evenly over 4 bread slices. Top each with a ham slice; top with remaining bread slices.

Spread half of butter on tops of sandwiches. Invert sandwiches onto a hot nonstick skillet or griddle, and cook over medium heat until browned. Spread remaining butter on ungrilled sides of sandwiches; turn and cook until browned. Yield: 4 servings.

GROCERIES NEEDED

Check staples: butter or margarine, all-purpose flour, salt, hot sauce, mayonnaise, prepared mustard

- 1 (4-ounce) jar diced pimiento
- 1 (14½-ounce) can ready-to-serve chicken broth
- 1½ cups half-and-half
- Small onion
- Sour cream
- 4 ounces Monterey Jack cheese
- 4 ounces Cheddar cheese
- 1 green onion
- 8 slices bread
- Sandwich ham

EQUIPMENT NEEDED

- Electric blender
- Heavy saucepan
- Nonstick skillet or griddle

MENU PLAN

1. Prepare soup; keep warm.

2. Assemble sandwiches; grill sandwiches just before serving.

Stir-Fry Night
Sweet Pepper-Chicken Stir-Fry
Grissini Breadsticks
Ice Cream with Chocolate Sauce

Serves 4

Sweet Pepper-Chicken Stir-Fry

PREP: 8 MINUTES   **COOK: 9 MINUTES**

TABLE TALK:

•Stir-fry sauce tends to be salty. That's why we recommend cooking the rice without added salt.

•Use boil-in-bag or instant rice to speed preparation.

•Grissini are long and very thin Italian breadsticks, slightly resembling chopsticks—edible ones.

1 to 2 tablespoons light sesame oil or vegetable oil
1 pound chicken breast strips (tenders)
2 tablespoons water
1 (16-ounce) package frozen broccoli, carrots, and cauliflower (stir-fry mix)

1 purple onion, cut into eight wedges
2 sweet red peppers, seeded and cut into thin strips
1 (11.75-ounce) bottle stir-fry sauce
Hot cooked rice (cooked without salt)

Pour oil around top of a preheated wok, coating sides, or in a large nonstick skillet. Heat at medium-high (375°) for 2 minutes. Add chicken, and stir-fry 2 minutes or until lightly browned.

Add water, frozen vegetables, onion, and red pepper strips, stirring gently. Cover and cook 6 minutes or until vegetables are crisp-tender, stirring once. Add stir-fry sauce; stir-fry 1 minute or until thoroughly heated. Serve over rice. Yield: 4 servings.

Alfresco Supper

Chicken Caesar Salad
Sliced Roma Tomatoes
Angel Food Cake with Berries and Cream

Serves 4

Chicken Caesar Salad

PREP: 10 MINUTES   **COOK: 6 MINUTES**

¼ cup white wine vinegar
2 teaspoons Dijon mustard
1 teaspoon Worcestershire
     sauce
1½ pounds chicken breast
     strips (tenders)
1½ tablespoons lemon-pepper
     seasoning

1 teaspoon garlic powder
¼ cup olive oil
8 cups tightly packed torn or
     shredded romaine lettuce
     (about 1 medium head)
2 cups garlic croutons
½ cup shredded Parmesan
     cheese

Combine first 3 ingredients, stirring well; set aside. Dredge chicken in lemon-pepper seasoning and garlic powder. Pour oil into a large skillet, and place over medium-high heat until hot. Cook chicken in hot oil 5 minutes or until done, turning once. Remove chicken from skillet, reserving drippings in skillet; drain chicken on paper towels. Remove skillet from heat; stir vinegar mixture into reserved drippings, scraping particles that cling to bottom of skillet. Pour warm vinegar dressing over lettuce; add chicken, and toss. Sprinkle with croutons and cheese. Yield: 4 servings.

TABLE TALK:

•This salad's almost a meal in itself. A glass of white wine and sliced juicy tomatoes add the sweet tang of summer.

•Chicken breast strips are sometimes labeled chicken tenders.

•For croutons, try a 5¼-ounce box of Old London Restaurant Style Garlic Croutons.

•Shredded Parmesan cheese comes in a bag and looks like it's freshly grated.

Spicy Spanish Supper
Jiffy Spanish Rice
Warm Flour Tortillas   Mixed Greens
Melon Slices and Red Grapes

Serves 4

Jiffy Spanish Rice

PREP: 5 MINUTES   COOK: 17 MINUTES

TABLE TALK:

•If you've got a jar of pimiento-stuffed olives in the refrigerator, chop some to sprinkle over this beefed-up rice dish.

•It takes only minutes to heat tortillas according to package directions in a skillet or microwave. Use the warm tortillas as scoopers for the spicy rice entrée.

1 pound ground chuck
1 (28-ounce) can whole tomatoes, undrained and chopped
1 tablespoon instant minced onion
2 tablespoons chili powder
½ teaspoon salt
½ teaspoon pepper
1 cup instant long-grain rice, uncooked
Garnish: pimiento-stuffed olives

Brown ground beef in a large skillet, stirring until it crumbles. Drain and return to skillet. Add tomato and next 4 ingredients, stirring well; bring to a boil. Add rice; cover, reduce heat, and simmer 5 minutes or until rice is tender. Garnish, if desired. Yield: 4 servings.

Microwave Directions: Crumble ground beef in a 2½-quart casserole. Cover with heavy-duty plastic wrap; fold back a corner of wrap to allow steam to escape. Microwave at HIGH 5 to 6 minutes; stir and drain. Add remaining ingredients. Cover and microwave at HIGH 10 to 12 minutes; stir. Let stand 5 to 10 minutes.

A German Feast

Kielbasa and Cabbage

Potato Salad   Sliced Beets

Pumpernickel Bread

Serves 4

Kielbasa and Cabbage

PREP: 7 MINUTES   COOK: 12 MINUTES

½ small cabbage, shredded
   (about 1 pound)
1½ pounds kielbasa sausage,
   cut into 1½-inch slices

1 teaspoon caraway seeds
¾ teaspoon seasoned salt
¼ cup commercial Italian
   salad dressing

Combine all ingredients in a large deep microwave-safe dish or large glass mixing bowl. Cover with heavy-duty plastic wrap; fold back a small corner of wrap to allow steam to escape.

Microwave at HIGH 12 minutes or until cabbage is tender, stirring once. Drain and serve immediately. Yield: 4 servings.

TABLE TALK:
•Kielbasa is also called Polish sausage.

•Stir one to two teaspoons celery seeds or caraway seeds into your potato salad to give it a German accent.

•Make time to toast and butter the brown bread just before dinner.

Griddle Dinner

Grilled Pizza Sandwiches
Tomato Soup
Brownies

Serves 4

Grilled Pizza Sandwiches

PREP: 12 MINUTES   COOK: 12 MINUTES

TABLE TALK:

•This sandwich is a pepperoni lover's dream. Choose a sturdy bread to contain it.

•Buy and heat two or three 10¾-ounce cans of tomato soup or your favorite soup to accompany the grilled sandwiches.

½ cup mayonnaise
2 teaspoons dried Italian seasoning
8 slices whole grain bread

6 ounces packaged sliced pepperoni
1½ cups (6 ounces) shredded mozzarella cheese

Combine mayonnaise and Italian seasoning; spread half of mixture evenly on 1 side of bread slices.

  Layer pepperoni and cheese on mayonnaise side of 4 bread slices; top with remaining bread slices, mayonnaise side down.

  Spread half of remaining mayonnaise mixture on tops of sandwiches. Place sandwiches, mayonnaise side down, in a hot griddle or large non-stick skillet. Cook over medium heat until bread is browned. Spread remaining mayonnaise mixture on ungrilled sides of sandwiches; turn and cook until sandwiches are browned. Yield: 4 servings.

Dinner Clamor
Quick Clam Linguine
Romaine Salad   Garlic Bread
Lemon Sherbet
Serves 2

Quick Clam Linguine

PREP: 5 MINUTES   COOK: 15 MINUTES

1 (9-ounce) package
    refrigerated linguine,
    uncooked
2 (6½-ounce) cans minced
    clams, undrained
¼ cup butter or margarine
5 cloves garlic, minced

½ cup whipping cream
1 cup (4 ounces) shredded
    Monterey Jack cheese
¼ cup chopped fresh parsley
    or 2 tablespoons dried
    parsley flakes

Cook pasta according to package directions; drain and set aside.
  Drain clams, reserving ¾ cup liquid. Set clams and liquid aside.
  Melt butter in a large skillet over medium-high heat; add garlic, and cook, stirring constantly, 1 minute. Add reserved clam liquid and cream. Bring to a boil; reduce heat, and simmer 11 minutes.
  Add clams; cook over low heat, stirring constantly, until heated. Pour over pasta; add cheese and parsley, and toss gently. Serve immediately. Yield: 2 servings.

TABLE TALK:
•Choose a robust commercial vinaigrette such as Ken's Balsamic Vinaigrette to top leaves of romaine lettuce.
•If you've got extra garlic on hand, rub a cut clove on French bread before toasting.

Fireside Supper

Tortilla-Chili Casserole
Mexicorn
Lettuce Wedges with Thousand Island Dressing
Coffee Ice Cream with Hot Fudge Topping

Serves 8

Tortilla-Chili Casserole

PREP: **7 MINUTES**   COOK: **20 MINUTES**

TABLE TALK:

•You can use two jars of queso cheese dip instead of the Cheddar soup in this casserole.

•Buy and heat three 11-ounce cans of Mexicorn in a saucepan to serve with the casserole.

1 (9-ounce) package tortilla chips, coarsely broken
2 (11-ounce) cans Cheddar soup, undiluted
2 (15-ounce) cans chunky chili with beans
Garnishes: sour cream, pickled jalapeño pepper slices

Place 4 cups broken chips in a lightly greased 13- x 9- x 2-inch baking dish; spread 1 can soup over chips. Spread chili over soup, and top with remaining can soup. Bake, uncovered, at 350° for 15 minutes. Sprinkle with remaining chips; bake 5 more minutes. Garnish, if desired. Yield: 8 servings.

Italian Sausage Dinner

Italian Sausage Sandwiches
Minestrone   Potato Chips

Serves 4

Italian Sausage Sandwiches

PREP: 5 MINUTES   COOK: 20 MINUTES

1 pound sweet or spicy Italian
  sausage in casings
1 medium-size green pepper,
  seeded and cut into strips
1 medium-size sweet red
  pepper, seeded and cut
  into strips
2 medium onions, cut into
  thin wedges

2 cloves garlic, minced
1 teaspoon fennel seeds
2 tablespoons water
4 (2-ounce) submarine loaves,
  split and toasted
1 cup (4 ounces) shredded
  mozzarella or provolone
  cheese

TABLE TALK:

•Submarine loaves are
also called hoagie rolls. Any
bun about six inches long
would be fine, actually, to
enclose these sizzling
sausages.

Cook sausage in a large skillet over medium-high heat 15 minutes or
until done, turning occasionally. Add green pepper strips and next 5
ingredients; cover and cook over medium heat 5 minutes or until
vegetables are tender, stirring often. Remove from heat.

  Place sausage on roll bottoms; top with vegetable mixture. Sprinkle
with cheese, and add roll tops. Serve immediately. Yield: 4 servings.

Shrimp on the Deck

Boiled Shrimp Supper
Tossed Salad Baguettes
Watermelon

Serves 4

Boiled Shrimp Supper

PREP: 3 MINUTES COOK: 20 MINUTES

3 quarts boiling water
4 (3-ounce) packages dry shrimp-and-crab boil seasoning*
1 teaspoon salt
1½ pounds new potatoes
1 (16-ounce) package frozen pearl or boiling onions

8 frozen half-ears whole kernel corn
2 lemons, cut in half
1½ pounds unpeeled large fresh shrimp
Lemon wedges
Cocktail sauce

Combine first 3 ingredients in a stockpot or large Dutch oven; bring to a boil. Add potatoes, frozen onions, frozen corn, and lemon halves; return to a boil, and cook 15 minutes or until potatoes are tender.

 Add shrimp; cover and cook 5 minutes or until shrimp turn pink. Drain mixture; remove and discard seasoning bags and lemon halves. Serve immediately with lemon wedges and cocktail sauce. Yield: 4 servings.
*For crab boil seasoning, we used Zatarain's.

Vegetarian Night
Black Beans and Yellow Rice
Tortilla Chips
Pineapple Chunks

Serves 3

Black Beans and Yellow Rice

PREP: 4 MINUTES   **COOK: 23 MINUTES**

- 1 (5-ounce) package saffron rice mix
- 1 (15-ounce) can black beans
- 3 tablespoons lime juice
- 1 teaspoon chili powder
- ½ teaspoon ground cumin
- 2 tablespoons chopped fresh cilantro, divided
- Garnishes: sour cream, sliced green onions

Cook rice according to package directions; keep warm.

  Meanwhile, drain beans, reserving 2 tablespoons liquid. Combine beans, reserved liquid, lime juice, chili powder, and cumin in a saucepan. Cook over medium heat until thoroughly heated; stir in 1 tablespoon cilantro. Serve beans over rice, and sprinkle with remaining 1 tablespoon cilantro. Garnish, if desired. Yield: 3 servings.

TABLE TALK:

• Tortilla chips add a crunchy dimension to this meatless meal. Look for red or blue chips, too.

• Toss a little chopped cilantro in with the canned pineapple, and serve it as a side dish. Or top it with flaked coconut, and make it dessert.

Sloppy Joe Supper

Sweet Sloppy Joes
Onion Rings   Fresh Fruit
Serves 4

Sweet Sloppy Joes

PREP: 5 MINUTES   **COOK: 23 MINUTES**

TABLE TALK:

•Some folks like their sloppy joes sweet. Some don't. You can omit the brown sugar in this recipe; it'll still taste great.

•Pop commercial frozen onion rings in the oven to bake while the sloppy joe mixture simmers. We liked Ore-Ida Onion Ringers with this menu.

•Slice some crisp apples to go on the side.

1½ pounds ground beef
1 small onion, chopped
1 small green pepper, seeded and chopped
1 (10¾-ounce) can tomato soup, undiluted
1 (8-ounce) can tomato sauce
1 cup ketchup

2 tablespoons brown sugar
1 tablespoon Worcestershire sauce
1 teaspoon prepared mustard
⅛ teaspoon garlic powder
4 sesame seed hamburger buns, toasted

Cook first 3 ingredients in a large skillet until beef is browned, stirring until it crumbles; drain. Stir in soup and next 6 ingredients; simmer 10 to 15 minutes, stirring often. Serve on toasted buns. Yield: 4 servings.

PAGE 97

PAGE 50

Easy Entrées

PAGE 100

PAGE 47

PICK FROM A POTPOURRI OF WELL-SEASONED BEEF AND CHICKEN RECIPES, CREAMY PASTAS, STIR-FRIES, AND MEGA-FLAVOR MEAT-LESS DISHES. OR HOW ABOUT ONE OF OUR DOZEN SLOW COOKER RECIPES? WITH VIRTUALLY NO WORK, YOU CAN COME HOME TO A JUICY MEAL THAT SIMMERED ALL DAY WITHOUT YOU.

PAGE 59

PAGE 80

Slow Cooker Sense

Time is on *your* side when you plug in your slow cooker. We've tested the slow cooker favorites on the next few pages on HIGH and LOW settings so they'll adapt to your schedule. If you work all day, cook long and slow on LOW. If you're home in the afternoon, cook on HIGH.

There's no secret to mastering the slow cooker, but here are some points to remember.

•**Slow cookers range in size** from one to six quarts. Some conveniently have a removable stoneware liner (bowl). The bowl is typically oven-proof and microwave safe. One-quart slow cookers have no HIGH or LOW setting—only off and on. Our recipes are developed for three- to four-quart cookers.

•**Read the instruction booklet** that comes with your particular slow cooker.

•**Fill the slow cooker at least half full** for best results.

•**There's no need to preheat** a slow cooker.

•**Generally, cook with the cover on,** and don't peek inside until it's time to stir. (There are exceptions for uncovering when thickening some sauces briefly at the end of cooking.)

•**For all-day cooking,** use the LOW setting.

•**One hour on HIGH equals** two- to two-and-a-half hours on LOW.

•**To make cleanup quick and easy,** coat the inside of the stoneware bowl with cooking spray.

•**Less is more.** Don't be alarmed by small amounts of liquid in ingredient lists of slow cooker recipes. Liquids don't boil away like they do with conventional cooking. Rather they accumulate from the meat and other ingredients, as well as from moisture that condenses inside the cooker. You'll usually have more liquid left at the end of slow cooking than you started with. If more liquid accumulates than desired, just drain it.

•**To convert a favorite recipe** to the slow cooker method, reduce the amount of liquid by half, unless you're preparing soup.

•**Add milk and other dairy products** near the end of the cooking time, or substitute an undiluted cream soup. (Some dairy products tend to separate during lengthy cooking.)

•**For maximum seasoning impact,** use whole leaf herbs and whole spices for all-day slow cooking. Add ground herbs and spices during the last hour of cooking for the most intense flavor.

•**Place vegetables in the slow cooker first,** and then add the meat.

•**There's no need to thaw** frozen vegetables for most slow cooker recipes.

•**To fit large pieces of meat** in your slow cooker, cut them into two or three pieces.

•**Use lean cuts of meat,** and trim visible fat to avoid a finished dish with excess grease floating on top.

•**For roasts and stews,** pour liquid over meat to moisten it. (And remember, more juices are retained here than are with conventional cooking.)

•**No fish story here.** Fish is not at its peak when cooked in the slow cooker. If you must, add it near the end of cooking to prevent it from falling apart.

•**Don't miss the Roasted Chicken** recipe on page 54. You can leave it unattended as it roasts, and it yields 4½ cups of chopped cooked meat for you to plug in to many of the chicken recipes throughout the book. You'll be one big step ahead for another dinner.

Peppered Beef Brisket in Beer

PREP: 10 MINUTES　　　**SLOW COOK: 4 TO 12 HOURS**

You can simmer this brisket up to 12 hours to suit your schedule. The nice thing is that the longer it simmers, the more tender it gets.
•Add mashed potatoes or toast to a plate of this tender peppered beef, and it becomes a filling meal.

1　large onion, sliced and separated into rings	½　cup chili sauce
1　(4-pound) beef brisket, trimmed	3　tablespoons brown sugar
¾　teaspoon pepper	2　cloves garlic, crushed
¾　cup beer	3　tablespoons all-purpose flour
	3　tablespoons water

Place onion rings in a 4-quart electric slow cooker. Sprinkle brisket with pepper. Place over onion rings in slow cooker. (Cut brisket in half to fit in slow cooker, if necessary.) Combine beer and next 3 ingredients; pour over brisket. Cover and cook on HIGH 4 to 6 hours or on LOW 8 to 12 hours.

　Remove brisket to a serving platter, reserving juices in slow cooker. Combine flour and water, stirring well; slowly whisk into juices in slow cooker. Cook, uncovered, on HIGH 5 minutes or until thickened, stirring often. Serve sauce over brisket. Yield: 10 servings.

Zippy Barbecue Pot Roast

PREP: 8 MINUTES　　　**SLOW COOK: 5 TO 9 HOURS**

•There's plenty of spicy sauce for this roast—serve some crusty French bread for soaking it up.

1½　teaspoons garlic salt	1　(12-ounce) bottle chili sauce
½　teaspoon pepper	2　tablespoons Worcestershire sauce
1　(4- to 5-pound) boneless chuck roast, trimmed	2　tablespoons hot sauce
2　tablespoons vegetable oil	3　tablespoons cornstarch
1　(12-ounce) can or 1 (10-ounce) bottle cola-flavored beverage	¼　cup water

Combine garlic salt and pepper; rub over roast. Brown roast on all sides in hot oil in a large skillet. Transfer roast to a 4-quart electric slow cooker. (Cut roast to fit in slow cooker, if necessary.) Combine cola and next 3 ingredients; pour over roast. Cover and cook on HIGH 5 to 6 hours or on LOW 8 to 9 hours. Remove roast from slow cooker, reserving juices in slow cooker; keep roast warm.

　Combine cornstarch and water, stirring well; stir into slow cooker. Cook, uncovered, on HIGH 15 minutes or until thickened, stirring occasionally. Serve sauce over roast. Yield: 8 to 12 servings.

Chuck Roast Barbecue

PREP: 10 MINUTES   SLOW COOK: 6 TO 9 HOURS

1 (2½-pound) boneless chuck roast, trimmed
2 medium onions, chopped
1 (12-ounce) can cola-flavored beverage (1½ cups)
⅓ cup Worcestershire sauce
1½ tablespoons apple cider vinegar or white vinegar
1½ teaspoons beef bouillon granules
¾ teaspoon dry mustard
¾ teaspoon chili powder
¼ to ½ teaspoon ground red pepper
3 cloves garlic, minced
1 cup ketchup
1 tablespoon butter or margarine
6 hamburger buns

Place roast in a 3½- or 4-quart electric slow cooker; add onion. Combine cola and next 7 ingredients; cover and chill 1 cup sauce. Pour remaining sauce over roast. Cover and cook on HIGH 6 hours or on LOW 9 hours or until roast is very tender. Remove roast with chopped onion from cooker, using a slotted spoon, and shred meat with two forks. (Reserve remaining meat juices to spoon over mashed potatoes or toast, if desired.)

Combine reserved sauce, ketchup, and butter in a saucepan; cook over medium heat, stirring constantly, until thoroughly heated. Pour sauce over shredded meat, stirring gently. Spoon meat mixture onto buns. Yield: 6 servings.

CHUCK ROAST BARBECUE

Roast Beef with Horseradish Sauce

PREP: 10 MINUTES   SLOW COOK: 8 TO 10 HOURS

•Eye-of-round is a lean piece of beef, and slow cooking it on LOW is the ideal method for tenderizing.

•Though no liquid goes into the slow cooker initially, meat juices will accumulate during cooking.

½ teaspoon garlic powder
½ teaspoon dried oregano
½ teaspoon dried thyme
½ teaspoon salt
½ teaspoon pepper
1 (3-pound) eye-of-round beef roast
Horseradish Sauce

Combine seasonings in a small bowl, and rub mixture over entire roast. Place roast in a 3- or 4-quart electric slow cooker. (Cut roast in half to fit in slow cooker, if necessary.) Cover and cook on LOW 8 to 10 hours.

Remove roast to a cutting board, reserving juices in slow cooker. Let roast stand 15 minutes; cut diagonally across the grain into thin slices. Serve with Horseradish Sauce and, if desired, *au jus* (with meat juices). Yield: 8 servings.

Horseradish Sauce

1 (8-ounce) carton sour cream
½ cup mayonnaise
1 tablespoon prepared horseradish
1 teaspoon beef bouillon granules
1 clove garlic, crushed, or ⅛ teaspoon garlic powder

Combine all ingredients in a small bowl; cover and chill, if desired. Yield: 1½ cups.

Beef Strips with Mushrooms and Peppers

PREP: 5 MINUTES   SLOW COOK: 3 TO 7 HOURS

1 (1-pound) top round steak, trimmed
1 (16-ounce) package frozen pepper stir-fry mix
1 (10³⁄₄-ounce) can condensed beefy mushroom soup, undiluted
1 (8-ounce) package sliced fresh mushrooms
1 (1-ounce) envelope onion soup mix
Hot cooked rice

• This oriental dish becomes very juicy as it slow cooks — it's more like a soup than a stir-fry. You may want to serve it in bowls.

Slice steak diagonally across the grain into thin strips. Combine steak, frozen stir-fry mix, and next 3 ingredients in a 3½- or 4-quart electric slow cooker, stirring well. Cover and cook on HIGH 3 to 4 hours or on LOW 6 to 7 hours. Serve over rice. Yield: 4 servings.

Spiced Pork

PREP: 15 MINUTES   SLOW COOK: 4 TO 10 HOURS

1 (2-pound) boneless pork loin roast, trimmed and cut into 2-inch pieces
2 (14½-ounce) cans whole tomatoes, drained and chopped
⅓ cup raisins
2 tablespoons tomato paste
2 tablespoons apple cider vinegar or white vinegar
1 tablespoon chopped pickled jalapeño peppers
1 teaspoon beef bouillon granules
¼ teaspoon salt
¼ teaspoon ground cinnamon
⅛ teaspoon ground cloves
1 large onion, chopped
Hamburger buns (optional)

• A subtle aroma of cinnamon and cloves will fill your kitchen as this piquant pork mixture simmers.

Combine all ingredients, except buns, in a 4-quart electric slow cooker, stirring well. Cover and cook on HIGH 4 to 5 hours or on LOW 8 to 10 hours.

  Remove pork from slow cooker, using a slotted spoon; let cool slightly. Shred pork, using two large forks. Return shredded pork to slow cooker; cook until thoroughly heated. Serve on toasted buns, if desired. Yield: 6 to 8 servings.

SWEET JALAPEÑO RIBS

Sweet Jalapeño Ribs

PREP: 30 MINUTES   SLOW COOK: 5½ TO 10½ HOURS

- Jalapeño jelly is a key ingredient in this recipe; it melts into a sweet-spicy glaze that coats these ribs and beans.

- Country-style ribs are extra meaty. If they come as a slab, you'll need to cut them apart to fit them in the slow cooker.

- Broiling the ribs first browns them, adds rich flavor, and removes excess fat.

2 (16-ounce) cans pinto beans, drained
3 pounds country-style pork ribs, trimmed
½ teaspoon garlic powder
½ teaspoon salt
½ teaspoon pepper

1 medium onion, chopped
1 (10.5-ounce) jar red jalapeño jelly
1 (5-ounce) bottle steak sauce*
2 jalapeño peppers, seeded and finely chopped (optional)

Place beans in a 4-quart electric slow cooker. Set aside.

Cut ribs apart; sprinkle with garlic powder, salt, and ½ teaspoon pepper. Place ribs on a rack in a broiler pan. Broil 5½ inches from heat (with electric oven door partially opened) 18 to 20 minutes or until well browned, turning once. Add ribs to slow cooker, and sprinkle with onion.

Combine jelly, steak sauce, and, if desired, chopped pepper in a saucepan; cook over low heat until jelly melts. Pour over ribs; stir gently.

Cover and cook on HIGH 5 to 6 hours or on LOW 9 to 10 hours. Remove ribs; skim fat from sauce. Cook sauce with beans, uncovered, on HIGH 30 more minutes or until slightly thickened. Add ribs just before serving to reheat. Yield: 4 servings.

*For steak sauce, we used A-1.

Texas Stew

PREP: 5 MINUTES

SLOW COOK: ABOUT 5½ TO 10½ HOURS

2 pounds beef tips, cut into
    1-inch pieces
1 (14½-ounce) can Mexican-
    style stewed tomatoes,
    undrained
1 (10½-ounce) can condensed
    beef broth, undiluted
1 (8-ounce) jar medium or
    mild picante sauce
1 (10-ounce) package frozen
    whole kernel corn

3 carrots, scraped and cut into
    ½-inch slices
1 medium onion, cut into thin
    wedges
2 cloves garlic, minced
1 teaspoon ground cumin
½ teaspoon salt
⅓ cup water
¼ cup all-purpose flour

• Sop up this Western stew with Sour Cream Cornbread (page 193).

Combine first 10 ingredients in a 3- or 4-quart electric slow cooker. Cover and cook on HIGH 5 hours or on LOW 10 hours or until meat is tender.

Combine water and flour, stirring until smooth; stir into meat mixture in slow cooker. Cook stew, uncovered, on HIGH 15 minutes or until thickened, stirring often. Yield: 10 cups.

Green Chile Soup

•Use 1½ pounds boneless beef cubes instead of chicken, if desired. Or use any type of ground meat; just brown it in a skillet beforehand.

1½ pounds skinned and boned chicken breast halves, cut into 1-inch cubes
3 (4.5-ounce) cans chopped green chiles, undrained
1 (15-ounce) can pinto beans, undrained
1 (14½-ounce) can stewed tomatoes, undrained
2 cups water
1 teaspoon salt
¼ teaspoon ground cumin
¼ teaspoon dried oregano
1 large onion, chopped
1 clove garlic, crushed
Toppings: sour cream, shredded Cheddar cheese, chopped avocado, sliced green onions

Place first 10 ingredients in a 3½- or 4-quart electric slow cooker. Cover and cook on HIGH 4 to 6 hours or on LOW 8 hours. Serve soup with desired toppings. Yield: 10 cups.

GREEN CHILE SOUP

Saucy Drumsticks and Thighs

PREP: 13 MINUTES   SLOW COOK: 3½ TO 6½ HOURS

1 (14½-ounce) can diced
    tomatoes with roasted
    garlic, undrained
1 (6-ounce) can tomato paste
¼ cup dried chopped onion or
    1 small onion, chopped
2 teaspoons chicken bouillon
    granules
1 teaspoon dried Italian
    seasoning

½ teaspoon salt
½ teaspoon garlic powder
½ teaspoon dried crushed red
    pepper
6 chicken drumsticks, skinned
6 chicken thighs, skinned
Hot cooked rice or egg noodles

•This is fall-off-the-bone-tender chicken after it simmers in a well-seasoned, thick tomato sauce.

•Use all chicken thighs, if you'd prefer.

Combine first 8 ingredients in a 4-quart electric slow cooker; add chicken pieces, pushing them down into sauce. Cover and cook on HIGH 3½ to 4 hours or on LOW 6½ hours. Serve over rice or noodles. Yield: 6 servings.

Chicken Barbecue

PREP: 5 MINUTES   SLOW COOK: 3½ TO 7 HOURS

1 medium onion, sliced
½ lemon, sliced and seeded
6 skinned chicken breast
    halves
1 (18-ounce) bottle thick
    barbecue sauce

½ cup cola-flavored beverage
¼ cup all-purpose flour
¼ cup water

•Choose a thick barbecue sauce to coat this chicken. It's a juicy recipe, and the thicker the sauce, the better.

Place onion and lemon slices in a 3½- or 4-quart electric slow cooker. Add chicken. Combine barbecue sauce and cola; pour over chicken. Cover and cook on HIGH 3½ to 4 hours or on LOW 7 hours. Remove chicken to a serving platter, reserving sauce in slow cooker (but discarding lemon).

  Combine flour and water, stirring well with a wire whisk; stir into sauce in slow cooker. Cook, uncovered, on HIGH 10 minutes or until sauce is thickened, stirring twice. Spoon sauce over chicken. Yield: 6 servings.

Roasted Chicken

PREP: 10 MINUTES   SLOW COOK: 4 TO 8 HOURS

•No liquid's added and no tending's required when roasting this whole chicken.

•Let this flavorful roasted bird cool completely, and then chop the meat to use in recipes throughout the book that call for chopped cooked chicken.

•Save the juices that accumulate in the slow cooker for making soup. Just skim off the fat.

1 (4- to 5-pound) roasting chicken
Salt and pepper
1 teaspoon lemon-pepper seasoning

½ teaspoon salt
½ teaspoon dried thyme
¼ to ½ teaspoon paprika
2 tablespoons olive oil
1 large clove garlic, minced

Remove giblets from chicken. Remove as much fat and skin as possible. Rinse and drain chicken; pat dry. Sprinkle cavity of chicken generously with salt and pepper.

Combine lemon-pepper seasoning and remaining 5 ingredients. Rub mixture all over chicken, coating the top well. Place chicken, breast side up, in a 4-quart electric slow cooker. Cover and cook on HIGH 4 to 5 hours or on LOW 7 to 8 hours. Remove chicken from slow cooker, and let cool to touch. Remove meat from bones, and chop. Yield: 4½ cups chopped cooked chicken.

Steak in Pepper Cream

PREP: 3 MINUTES   COOK: 19 MINUTES

•Find green peppercorns in small jars on the grocery shelf along with pickles.

¼ teaspoon salt
2 (12-ounce) New York strip steaks (¾ inch thick)
1½ tablespoons green peppercorns in liquid, drained

2 tablespoons steak sauce
2 tablespoons water
1 cup whipping cream
¼ teaspoon ground pepper

Place a 10-inch cast-iron skillet over medium heat until hot; sprinkle salt in skillet. Place steaks over salt; cook 4 minutes on each side or until browned. Remove from skillet.

Combine peppercorns, steak sauce, and water in hot skillet; cook over medium heat, stirring constantly, to loosen any browned bits in bottom of skillet. Stir in whipping cream and pepper.

Bring to a boil; reduce heat, and simmer, stirring constantly, 3 to 4 minutes or until slightly thickened. Add steaks; simmer 5 minutes or to desired doneness, stirring occasionally. Yield: 2 to 4 servings.

Garlic Grilled Steak

PREP: 5 MINUTES   MARINATE: 8 TO 12 HOURS

GRILL: 20 MINUTES

¼ cup red wine vinegar
¼ cup soy sauce
¼ cup vegetable oil
¼ teaspoon freshly ground
    pepper

2 large cloves garlic, sliced
1 (2-pound) top round steak
    (1½ to 2 inches thick)
¼ teaspoon salt

•Vinegar's acidity helps tenderize the meat, while sliced garlic infuses it with great flavor.

Combine first 5 ingredients in a heavy-duty, zip-top plastic bag. Add steak, turning to coat. Seal bag; marinate in refrigerator 8 to 12 hours, turning occasionally.

  Remove steak from marinade, reserving marinade. Place marinade in a saucepan; bring to a boil. Remove from heat.

  Grill steak, covered with grill lid, over medium-hot coals (350° to 400°) 8 to 10 minutes on each side or to desired doneness, basting occasionally with reserved marinade. Remove from grill, and let stand 5 minutes; sprinkle with salt. Cut steak diagonally across the grain into thin slices. Yield: 6 servings.

Steak Soft Tacos

PREP: 6 MINUTES   MARINATE: 8 HOURS

GRILL: 10 MINUTES

½ cup vegetable oil
3 tablespoons lemon juice
3 tablespoons grated onion
1 tablespoon white wine
    vinegar or white vinegar
2 teaspoons chili powder

2 teaspoons dried oregano
1 teaspoon ground cumin
½ teaspoon garlic salt
2 pounds sirloin steak
10 (8-inch) flour tortillas
Salsa

•Stop by the salad bar at your local grocery store for favorite toppings to pile on these tacos.

•You can make **Chicken Soft Tacos** by coating two pounds of skinned and boned chicken breast halves with the first eight ingredients. Marinate and grill as directed.

Combine first 8 ingredients in a large heavy-duty, zip-top plastic bag; add steak. Seal bag; marinate in refrigerator 8 hours, turning often.

  Remove steak from marinade, discarding marinade. Grill steak, covered with grill lid, over medium-hot coals (350° to 400°) 5 minutes on each side or to desired doneness. Cut steak diagonally across the grain into strips.

  Heat tortillas according to package directions. Place steak down center of each tortilla; fold sides of each tortilla over steak. Serve with salsa. Yield: 5 servings.

Steak Stroganoff with Parslied Noodles

PREP: 7 MINUTES   COOK: 26 MINUTES

•No time to make Parslied Noodles? Just buy a package of egg noodles, and cook according to package directions.

1 medium onion, thinly sliced and separated into rings
1 tablespoon vegetable oil
¼ cup all-purpose flour
1 teaspoon salt
4 (4-ounce) cubed steaks

2 tablespoons vegetable oil
1 (4-ounce) can mushroom stems and pieces, undrained
½ cup sour cream
Parslied Noodles

Cook onion in 1 tablespoon oil in a large skillet over medium-high heat 5 minutes or until onion is tender, stirring often. Remove onion, and set aside.

Combine flour and salt; dredge steaks in flour mixture. Heat 2 tablespoons oil in skillet; add steaks. Cover and cook over medium heat 4 minutes on each side or until done. Remove steaks, and keep warm. Add onion and mushrooms to pan drippings; cook until thoroughly heated. Remove from heat, and stir in sour cream.

Arrange steaks over Parslied Noodles, and spoon sauce over steaks. Yield: 4 servings.

Parslied Noodles

4 cups water
2 teaspoons salt
4 ounces wide egg noodles, uncooked
1 tablespoon butter or margarine

1 tablespoon chopped fresh parsley or 1 teaspoon dried parsley flakes

Combine water and salt; bring to a boil. Add noodles, and cook 7 to 9 minutes, stirring occasionally; drain. Combine noodles, butter, and parsley. Yield: 4 servings.

Quick Beef with Broccoli

PREP: 18 MINUTES   COOK: 7 MINUTES

½ pound boneless top round
    or flank steak, trimmed
10 dried tomato slices or
    halves (packed without oil)
¾ cup boiling water
2 teaspoons cornstarch
¼ cup soy sauce
1½ teaspoons sugar

Vegetable cooking spray
2 cups fresh broccoli flowerets
    or 1 (10-ounce) package
    frozen broccoli flowerets,
    thawed
3 green onions, sliced
1 clove garlic, minced
Hot cooked rice

• This is an easy dinner for two. Plug in the electric wok, if you have one.

Slice steak diagonally across the grain into very thin slices.

  Combine tomato slices and boiling water; let stand 5 minutes. Drain and slice tomato into thin strips, reserving liquid.

  Combine cornstarch, soy sauce, sugar, and reserved liquid, stirring until smooth. Set aside.

  Coat a large nonstick skillet with cooking spray; place over medium-high heat until hot. Add steak, and cook, stirring constantly, 3 minutes. Remove from skillet, and set aside. Add tomato strips, broccoli, green onions, and garlic. Cook, stirring constantly, 3 minutes. Add cornstarch mixture and steak, and cook, stirring constantly, 1 minute. Serve over rice. Yield: 2 servings.

Beef-Stuffed Peppers

PREP: 13 MINUTES   **COOK: 16 MINUTES**

•We prefer ground round for this recipe. It's lean enough to stuff into the peppers without cooking and draining it first.

4   medium-size green peppers
1   large egg, lightly beaten
1   (14-ounce) jar spaghetti
     sauce, divided
1   cup seasoned croutons,
     crushed

1   teaspoon dried onion flakes
¼   teaspoon pepper
¾   pound ground round
Grated Parmesan cheese

Cut off tops of peppers, and remove seeds and membranes.

Combine egg, ¾ cup spaghetti sauce, and next 4 ingredients. Stuff peppers with meat mixture; place peppers in a lightly greased 8-inch square baking dish. Cover loosely with wax paper.

Microwave at HIGH 12 to 14 minutes, giving dish a half-turn after 6 minutes. Spoon 1 tablespoon spaghetti sauce over each pepper. Sprinkle with Parmesan cheese. Heat remaining spaghetti sauce, and serve with peppers. Yield: 4 servings.

Green Chile Enchiladas

PREP: 15 MINUTES   **COOK: 32 MINUTES**

1½ pounds ground chuck
1   small onion, chopped
1   (10¾-ounce) can cream of
     mushroom soup, undiluted
2   (4.5-ounce) cans chopped
     green chiles, undrained
8   (8- or 9-inch) flour tortillas

1   (8-ounce) package shredded
     colby-Monterey Jack
     cheese blend, divided
1   (10¾-ounce) can Cheddar
     cheese soup, undiluted
Salsa

Brown ground chuck and onion in a large skillet, stirring until meat crumbles; drain. Stir in mushroom soup and 1 can green chiles.

Spoon about ½ cup beef mixture down center of each tortilla; sprinkle each with 2½ tablespoons shredded cheese. Roll up tortillas; place, seam side down, in a lightly greased 13- x 9- x 2-inch baking dish. Stir remaining can green chiles into Cheddar soup. Spoon mixture over tortillas, spreading to edges. Sprinkle remaining shredded cheese over enchiladas.

Cover and bake at 350° for 20 minutes; uncover and bake 5 more minutes. Serve with salsa. Yield: 4 servings.

Arabic Rice

1½ pounds ground chuck

3 tablespoons garlic powder

2 tablespoons ground
cinnamon

1 tablespoon ground allspice

2 cups long-grain rice,
uncooked

1 tablespoon beef bouillon
granules

4 cups water

¼ cup pine nuts, toasted

2 green onions, chopped

Rice wine vinegar or lemon
juice

Combine first 4 ingredients in a large skillet; cook over medium heat until meat is browned, stirring until it crumbles. Stir in rice, bouillon granules, and water.

  Bring to a boil. Cover, reduce heat, and cook 25 minutes or until liquid is absorbed and rice is tender. Sprinkle with pine nuts and green onions; serve with rice wine vinegar. Yield: 4 to 6 servings.

•Yes, the amounts of garlic powder and spices are correct for this highly seasoned Middle Eastern entrée.

•A crisp tossed salad and warm pita bread are nice additions for this ethnic dish, and raisins and chutney are traditional condiments to top it off.

•If you can't find pine nuts in the grocery store, use pecans.

ARABIC RICE

Oriental Burgers

PREP: 11 MINUTES   GRILL: 12 MINUTES

1 pound ground chuck
⅓ cup chopped water chestnuts
¼ cup chopped green pepper
1 tablespoon brown sugar
2 tablespoons water
1 tablespoon lemon juice
1 tablespoon soy sauce
½ teaspoon ground ginger

2 green onions, finely chopped
Vegetable cooking spray
4 sesame seed hamburger buns
Lettuce leaves
1 small white or purple onion, sliced
Hoisin Ketchup

Combine first 9 ingredients; shape into 4 patties.

Coat grill rack with cooking spray; place rack on grill over medium-hot coals (350° to 400°). Place patties on rack; grill, uncovered, 5 to 6 minutes on each side or until done.

Place patties on buns with lettuce and onion. Spoon Hoisin Ketchup evenly over burgers. Yield: 4 servings.

Hoisin Ketchup

¼ cup ketchup   ¼ cup hoisin sauce

Combine ketchup and hoisin sauce. Yield: ½ cup.

ORIENTAL
BURGERS

Hamburgers Teriyaki

PREP: 5 MINUTES   COOK: 20 MINUTES

1½ pounds ground beef
3 tablespoons teriyaki or soy
  sauce
1 tablespoon honey
1 teaspoon salt

¾ teaspoon ground ginger
2 cloves garlic, minced
4 hamburger buns, toasted
Lettuce leaves
Tomato slices

Combine first 6 ingredients; shape into 4 patties. Cook patties in a large skillet over medium-low heat 20 minutes, turning once.

  Place patties on buns with lettuce and tomato; serve with mayonnaise and mustard. Yield: 4 servings.

•Spread a little Chinese mustard on these burgers for a tangy surprise.

•Cooking the burgers over medium-low heat keeps the honey in them from burning.

Little Meat Loaves

PREP: 5 MINUTES   COOK: 30 MINUTES

1½ pounds ground beef
2 (8-ounce) cans tomato sauce,
  divided
1 cup soft breadcrumbs
2 tablespoons dried minced
  onion flakes
¾ teaspoon salt

¼ teaspoon pepper
2 large eggs, lightly beaten
2 teaspoons dried parsley
  flakes
1 teaspoon Worcestershire
  sauce

Combine ground beef, ½ cup tomato sauce, and next 5 ingredients; stir well. Shape mixture into 6 loaves. Place loaves on a greased rack of a broiler pan. Bake loaves, uncovered, at 450° for 25 minutes or to desired doneness.

  Combine remaining tomato sauce, parsley flakes, and Worcestershire sauce. Remove pan from oven; pour tomato mixture over meat loaves. Bake 5 more minutes. Yield: 6 servings.

•Line your broiler pan with foil for easy cleanup.

Upside-Down Pizza

PREP: 4 MINUTES   COOK: 35 MINUTES

•Servings are easy to measure for this pizza casserole; just follow the natural perforations in the crescent rolls.

2 pounds ground chuck
1 cup chopped onion
1 (15-ounce) can tomato sauce
1 (1¼-ounce) envelope spaghetti sauce mix

1 (8-ounce) carton sour cream
2 cups (8 ounces) shredded mozzarella cheese
1 (8-ounce) can refrigerated crescent rolls

Brown ground chuck and onion in a large skillet over medium-high heat, stirring until meat crumbles; drain and return to skillet. Stir in tomato sauce and spaghetti sauce mix; cook over low heat 10 minutes, stirring often.

Spoon beef mixture into a lightly greased 13- x 9- x 2-inch baking dish; top with sour cream, and sprinkle with cheese. Unroll crescent rolls, and place over cheese. Bake, uncovered, at 350° for 20 to 25 minutes. Yield: 8 servings.

Speedy Spaghetti

PREP: 5 MINUTES   COOK: 25 MINUTES

8 ounces dried spaghetti, uncooked
1 pound ground beef
1 small onion, chopped
2 (14½-ounce) cans Italian-style diced tomatoes, undrained

2 (6-ounce) cans tomato paste
2 teaspoons dried Italian seasoning
1 teaspoon sugar

Cook pasta according to package directions; drain.

Meanwhile, brown ground beef and chopped onion in a large skillet over medium heat, stirring until meat crumbles; drain and return to skillet. Stir in tomatoes and remaining 3 ingredients. Cook over medium heat 20 minutes, stirring occasionally. Serve over pasta. Yield: 4 servings.

Variation: For **Slow Cooker Spaghetti,** just place cooked ground beef and remaining ingredients, except spaghetti, in a 3½-quart electric slow cooker. Cover and cook on LOW 5 hours. Uncover and add 1½ cups hot water. Break spaghetti, and add to slow cooker. Cover and cook 1 hour on HIGH. Just before serving, stir in 1 cup of shredded cheese, if desired.

Shortcut Lasagna

1 pound ground beef
2 large cloves garlic, crushed
1 (28-ounce) jar spaghetti
   sauce
½ cup water
1 large egg, lightly beaten
1 (12-ounce) container cottage
   cheese
1½ teaspoons pepper

8 lasagna noodles, uncooked
1 (10-ounce) package frozen
   chopped spinach, thawed
   and drained
2 cups (8 ounces) shredded
   mozzarella cheese
½ cup grated Parmesan
   cheese

Crumble beef into a 2-quart glass bowl; add garlic. Microwave at HIGH 6 minutes or until browned, stirring beef once; drain. Stir in spaghetti sauce and water.

Combine egg, cottage cheese, and pepper.

Spread ½ cup meat sauce in a 13- x 9- x 2-inch baking dish. Top with half each of uncooked noodles, cottage cheese mixture, spinach, meat sauce, and mozzarella cheese. Repeat layers, and cover with heavy-duty plastic wrap.

Microwave at HIGH 8 minutes; then microwave at MEDIUM (50% power) 30 to 32 minutes or until noodles are tender, turning dish occasionally.

Sprinkle with Parmesan cheese; cover and let stand 15 minutes before serving. Yield: 6 servings.

•The shortcut? Not cooking the noodles before layering them. They soften as they bake in the lasagna.

•If your microwave won't hold a 13- x 9- x 2-inch dish, use your oven instead. Just cover the dish with foil, and bake at 350° for 50 minutes. Sprinkle with Parmesan cheese, and bake, uncovered, 10 more minutes. Let stand 10 minutes before serving.

Beef Burritos

PREP: 20 MINUTES   COOK: 35 MINUTES

1 pound ground beef
2 cloves garlic, minced
1 small onion, chopped
1 jalapeño pepper, seeded and minced, or 2 tablespoons chopped pickled jalapeño pepper
1 small green pepper, seeded and chopped
1 cup water
1 tablespoon taco seasoning
8 (8- or 9-inch) flour tortillas
2 cups shredded lettuce
2 tomatoes, chopped
1 cup (4 ounces) shredded Cheddar cheese
1 (8-ounce) carton guacamole
Taco or picante sauce

Cook first 5 ingredients in a large skillet until meat is browned, stirring until it crumbles; drain well, and return to skillet. Stir in water and taco seasoning; bring to a boil. Cover, reduce heat, and simmer 20 minutes, stirring occasionally. Uncover and cook 5 more minutes.

Wrap tortillas in aluminum foil. Bake at 350° for 10 minutes or until heated. Spoon meat mixture evenly down centers of tortillas. Top with lettuce, tomato, cheese, guacamole, and taco sauce. Fold bottom third of each tortilla over filling. Fold sides of tortillas in toward center, and fold tops over. Serve with more taco sauce, if desired. Yield: 4 servings.

Mushroom-Veal Marsala

PREP: 6 MINUTES   COOK: 13 MINUTES

•Marsala is a smoky-flavored Italian wine. You can substitute ¼ cup dry white wine plus 1 teaspoon brandy for Marsala.

1 teaspoon chopped fresh or dried rosemary
½ teaspoon salt
½ teaspoon freshly ground pepper
1 pound (¼-inch-thick) veal scaloppine
2 tablespoons olive oil
1 (8-ounce) package sliced fresh mushrooms
2 cloves garlic, minced
2 teaspoons cornstarch
1 teaspoon chicken bouillon granules
⅔ cup water
⅓ cup dry Marsala

Rub first 3 ingredients over veal. Heat oil in a large nonstick skillet over medium heat. Add half of veal; cook 2 minutes on each side or until lightly browned. Remove veal from skillet; keep warm. Repeat with remaining veal.

Add mushrooms and garlic to skillet; cook over medium-high heat, stirring constantly, 3 minutes or until tender.

MUSHROOM-VEAL MARSALA

Combine cornstarch and remaining 3 ingredients; add to skillet. Cook, stirring constantly, 1 minute or until thick and bubbly. Serve over veal. Yield: 4 servings.

Veal Piccata

PREP: 10 MINUTES   COOK: 5 MINUTES

4 veal cutlets (about ¾ pound)
¼ cup all-purpose flour
½ teaspoon salt
½ teaspoon pepper
2 tablespoons peanut or
    vegetable oil

⅓ cup dry white wine
2 tablespoons butter or
    margarine
2 tablespoons lemon juice
2 teaspoons grated lemon rind
¼ cup chopped fresh parsley

Place veal between two sheets of heavy-duty plastic wrap; flatten to ⅛-inch thickness, using a meat mallet or rolling pin. Combine flour, salt, and pepper; dredge veal in flour mixture. Cook veal in oil in a large nonstick skillet over medium-high heat 1 minute on each side. Remove from skillet; keep warm.

  Add wine to hot skillet; cook over high heat, deglazing skillet by scraping bits that cling to bottom. Add butter and lemon juice; heat just until butter melts. Pour over veal, and sprinkle with lemon rind and parsley. Yield: 2 servings.

Lemon Pork on Fettuccine

PREP: 10 MINUTES   COOK: 10 MINUTES

•Look for tenderloins packed in a vacuum seal in the meat department.

•Capers are tangy green buds that resemble peppercorns. Find them in jars near other condiments in the grocery store.

2 (¾-pound) pork tenderloins
½ cup all-purpose flour
½ teaspoon salt
¼ teaspoon pepper
3 tablespoons olive oil
½ cup dry white wine
½ cup lemon juice

3 tablespoons butter or
    margarine
¼ cup chopped fresh parsley
1½ tablespoons capers
Hot cooked fettuccine
Garnishes: lemon slices, fresh
    parsley sprigs

Cut each pork tenderloin into 6 (2-ounce) medaillons. Place between two sheets of heavy-duty plastic wrap; flatten to ¼-inch thickness, using a meat mallet or rolling pin.

  Combine flour, salt, and pepper; dredge pork in flour mixture. Cook half of pork in 1½ tablespoons hot oil in a large skillet over medium heat 2 minutes on each side or until browned. Remove pork from skillet; keep warm. Repeat with remaining pork and 1½ tablespoons oil.

  Add wine and lemon juice to skillet; cook until heated. Add butter, chopped parsley, and capers; stir until butter melts. Serve pork over pasta; drizzle with wine mixture. Garnish, if desired. Yield: 4 to 6 servings.

MOLASSES-GRILLED PORK TENDERLOIN

Molasses-Grilled Pork Tenderloin

PREP: 5 MINUTES   MARINATE: 8 HOURS
GRILL: 20 MINUTES

½ cup molasses
¼ cup coarse-grained Dijon
    mustard
2 tablespoons apple cider
    vinegar or white vinegar

1 teaspoon salt
4 (¾-pound) pork tenderloins
Vegetable cooking spray

•Serve this darkly glazed grilled pork to company. Pair it with grilled vegetables and a spicy red wine.

•Looking for a shortcut? Grill the tenderloins as soon as you've glazed them. You don't have to marinate them.

Combine first 4 ingredients; brush half of mixture over pork. Cover and chill 8 hours. Chill remaining molasses glaze.

  Coat grill rack with cooking spray; place on grill over medium-hot coals (350° to 400°). Place pork on rack; grill, covered with grill lid, 18 to 20 minutes or until a meat thermometer inserted into thickest portion registers 160°, turning once and basting with reserved molasses glaze during last 8 minutes. Yield: 8 servings.

Sweet-and-Saucy Pork Chops

PREP: 5 MINUTES   COOK: 30 MINUTES

•If you don't have cinnamon applesauce, just stir ⅛ teaspoon ground cinnamon into ½ cup regular applesauce.

½ cup ketchup
¼ cup tomato juice or spicy vegetable juice
¼ cup finely chopped onion
3 tablespoons honey
2 tablespoons white vinegar
1 tablespoon Worcestershire sauce

1 teaspoon dry mustard
½ teaspoon coarsely ground pepper
½ cup cinnamon applesauce
4 center-cut pork chops

Combine first 8 ingredients in a saucepan; bring mixture to a boil over medium heat. Reduce heat; simmer, uncovered, 5 minutes. Stir in applesauce. Set aside ½ cup applesauce mixture; cook remaining mixture, uncovered, over low heat 15 minutes, stirring occasionally.

  Place pork chops on lightly greased rack of a broiler pan, and brush with ¼ cup of reserved applesauce mixture. Broil 5½ inches from heat (with electric oven door partially opened) 5 minutes. Turn and brush pork chops with remaining ¼ cup reserved applesauce mixture. Broil 5 more minutes or until done. Transfer to a serving platter; spoon heated applesauce mixture over pork. Yield: 4 servings.

Peachy Pork Chops

PREP: 5 MINUTES   COOK: 24 MINUTES

4 (1-inch-thick) pork chops
¼ teaspoon seasoned salt
¼ teaspoon onion powder
1 (16-ounce) can sliced peaches, undrained

2 tablespoons brown sugar
2 tablespoons butter or margarine
½ teaspoon dried basil

Place pork on a lightly greased rack of a broiler pan. Sprinkle with salt and onion powder. Broil 5½ inches from heat (with electric oven door partially opened) 7 minutes on each side or to desired doneness.

  Combine peaches and remaining 3 ingredients in a saucepan. Cook, uncovered, over low heat 10 minutes, stirring often. Arrange pork chops on a platter. Pour peach sauce over pork. Yield: 4 servings.

Pork Chops with Baked Beans

PREP: 5 MINUTES   COOK: 45 MINUTES

1 (16-ounce) can pork and
  beans
½ cup chopped onion
¼ cup firmly packed brown
  sugar
½ cup ketchup, divided

1 teaspoon prepared mustard
4 (½-inch-thick) boneless
  pork chops
1 tablespoon brown sugar
1 teaspoon Worcestershire
  sauce

Combine pork and beans, onion, ¼ cup brown sugar, ¼ cup ketchup, and mustard in a lightly greased 2-quart baking dish. Arrange pork chops over bean mixture.

  Combine remaining ¼ cup ketchup, 1 tablespoon brown sugar, and Worcestershire sauce; spread on pork chops. Cover and bake at 350° for 25 minutes. Uncover and bake 20 more minutes. Yield: 4 servings.

Kung Pao Pork

PREP: 13 MINUTES   COOK: 8 MINUTES

⅓ cup water
¼ cup soy sauce
2½ tablespoons sugar
1 tablespoon lemon juice
2 teaspoons cornstarch
¼ teaspoon dried crushed red
  pepper
2 tablespoons peanut or
  vegetable oil

¾ pound lean boneless pork
  loin, cut into ½-inch cubes
2 large cloves garlic, minced
1 small sweet red or green
  pepper, cut into thin strips
1 small onion, cut into wedges
¼ cup unsalted roasted
  peanuts
Hot cooked rice

Combine first 6 ingredients in a bowl, stirring with a whisk until blended; set aside.

  Pour oil around top of a preheated wok, coating sides, or in a large non-stick skillet; heat at medium-high (375°) 1 minute. Add pork and garlic; stir-fry 3 minutes or until pork is lightly browned. Add pepper strips and onion; stir-fry 3 minutes or until vegetables are tender.

  Stir in soy sauce mixture; cook, stirring constantly, 1 minute or until thickened. Stir in peanuts. Serve over rice. Yield: 2 to 3 servings.

Sesame Pork Linguine

PREP: 16 MINUTES   COOK: 8 MINUTES

•Dark sesame oil has a strong, distinct flavor. Any oil will substitute fine in this recipe, but the flavor of the dish will be much milder.

•Find dark sesame oil with other oils or Asian ingredients in the supermarket.

8 ounces dried linguine, uncooked
¼ cup all-purpose flour
½ teaspoon salt
¼ teaspoon pepper
1 pound lean boneless pork loin, cut into thin 3-inch-long strips
Vegetable cooking spray
¼ cup dark sesame oil, divided

¼ cup sesame seeds
3 tablespoons soy sauce
2 tablespoons rice or white vinegar
6 green onions, cut into 1½-inch strips
2 tablespoons sesame seeds, toasted

Cook pasta according to package directions; drain and keep warm.

Combine flour, salt, and pepper in a large heavy-duty, zip-top plastic bag. Place pork in bag; seal bag, and shake until pork is coated.

Coat a large nonstick skillet with cooking spray; add 1 tablespoon sesame oil. Place over medium-high heat until hot. Add pork; stir-fry 3 to 4 minutes or until done. Remove pork from skillet, and set aside.

Combine ¼ cup sesame seeds and remaining 3 tablespoons oil in container of an electric blender; cover and process until seeds are ground, stopping to scrape down sides. Transfer mixture to skillet; stir in soy sauce, vinegar, and green onions. Cook over medium heat 1 minute, stirring often.

Return pork to skillet, and cook until thoroughly heated. Toss with hot cooked pasta, sprinkle with toasted sesame seeds, and serve hot. Yield: 4 servings.

HUNAN PORK AND ZUCCHINI STIR-FRY

Hunan Pork and Zucchini Stir-Fry

PREP: 11 MINUTES   COOK: 10 MINUTES

¼ cup cornstarch
¼ cup water
1 pound boneless pork, cut into thin strips
3 tablespoons vegetable oil, divided

3 small zucchini, sliced (about 3 cups)
⅓ cup Hunan sauce*
1 tablespoon sesame seeds, toasted
Hot cooked rice

•If you can't find Hunan sauce at a cook store or specialty grocery store, substitute hoisin sauce or a stir-fry sauce.

Combine cornstarch and water, stirring until smooth. Add pork, tossing well. Heat 2 tablespoons oil in a large skillet over medium-high heat until hot. Add pork mixture; stir-fry 3 minutes or until pork is no longer pink. Remove from skillet. Heat remaining 1 tablespoon oil in skillet. Add zucchini; stir-fry 3 minutes or until tender.

Return pork to skillet; add Hunan sauce and sesame seeds. Stir-fry until thoroughly heated. Serve over rice. Yield: 4 servings.

*For Hunan sauce, we used Wei Chuan. It's spicy.

Tex-Mex Egg Burritos

PREP: 12 MINUTES   COOK: 13 MINUTES

4 (8-inch) flour tortillas
½ pound hot ground pork
    sausage
6 large eggs, lightly beaten

1 (4.5-ounce) can chopped
    green chiles, undrained
Picante sauce
Shredded Cheddar cheese

Heat tortillas according to package directions.

  Meanwhile, brown sausage in a large skillet, stirring until it crumbles; drain and return to skillet. Add eggs and chiles to sausage. Cook, without stirring, until mixture begins to set on bottom. Draw a spatula across bottom of pan to form large curds. Continue cooking until eggs are thickened but still moist. Do not stir constantly.

  Spoon egg mixture evenly down centers of warm tortillas; top each with picante sauce and cheese. Fold opposite sides over filling. Serve immediately. Yield: 4 servings.

Creamy Ham Casserole

PREP: 10 MINUTES   COOK: 35 MINUTES

4 ounces medium egg noodles,
    uncooked
2 cups chopped cooked ham
1 medium-size green pepper,
    seeded and chopped
¼ cup chopped onion
¼ cup sliced celery

1 tablespoon vegetable oil
1 (10¾-ounce) can cream of
    mushroom soup, undiluted
1 (8-ounce) carton sour cream
½ cup (2 ounces) shredded
    Cheddar cheese

Cook pasta according to package directions; drain.

  Cook ham and next 3 ingredients in oil in a large skillet over medium-high heat 5 minutes, stirring often. Remove from heat; stir in soup, sour cream, and pasta. Spoon into a lightly greased 1½-quart baking dish.

  Cover and bake at 350° for 25 minutes. Sprinkle with cheese, and bake, uncovered, 5 more minutes. Let stand 10 minutes before serving. Yield: 4 servings.

Ham and Grits Crustless Quiche

PREP: 15 MINUTES   COOK: 35 MINUTES

½ cup water
¼ teaspoon salt
⅓ cup quick-cooking yellow grits, uncooked
1 (12-ounce) can evaporated milk
1½ cups chopped cooked ham

1 cup (4 ounces) shredded sharp Cheddar cheese
1 tablespoon chopped fresh parsley
1 teaspoon dry mustard
1 to 2 teaspoons hot sauce
3 large eggs, lightly beaten

Bring water and salt to a boil in a large saucepan; stir in grits. Remove from heat; cover and let stand 5 minutes (mixture will be thick). Stir in milk and remaining ingredients. Pour into a lightly greased 9½-inch quiche dish or deep-dish pieplate.

Bake at 350° for 30 to 35 minutes. Let stand 10 minutes before serving. Yield: 4 to 6 servings.

•This recipe's for when you're in a "breakfast-for-dinner" mood.

Ham and Potato Casserole

PREP: 10 MINUTES   COOK: 30 MINUTES

1 (26-ounce) package frozen shredded potatoes
1 (1-pound) ham slice, cut into bite-size pieces (2½ cups)
1 (10¾-ounce) can cream of potato soup, undiluted

½ teaspoon pepper
¼ cup grated Parmesan cheese
1 cup (4 ounces) shredded sharp Cheddar cheese
Paprika

Combine first 4 ingredients; spoon mixture into a lightly greased 13- x 9- x 2-inch baking dish. Bake, uncovered, at 400° for 25 minutes; sprinkle with cheeses and paprika. Bake 5 more minutes or until thoroughly heated. Yield: 4 to 6 servings.

•You can use just about any canned "cream of" soup in this versatile casserole.

Grilled Ham and Apples

PREP: 7 MINUTES   GRILL: 10 MINUTES

½ cup orange marmalade
2 teaspoons butter or
   margarine
¼ teaspoon ground ginger
Vegetable cooking spray

2 (½-inch-thick) ham slices
   (about 2½ pounds)
4 small Granny Smith apples,
   cored and cut into 4 rings
   each

Combine first 3 ingredients in a 1-cup glass measuring cup; microwave at HIGH 1 minute or until melted, stirring once.

  Coat grill rack with cooking spray; place on grill over medium-hot coals (350° to 400°). Place ham and apple rings on rack; grill, uncovered, 10 minutes or until apple rings are tender, turning and basting often with marmalade mixture. Yield: 6 to 8 servings.

GRILLED HAM AND APPLES

Hot Brown Pasta Casserole

PREP: 15 MINUTES   COOK: 45 MINUTES

4 ounces penne pasta,
    uncooked (2½ cups
    cooked)
6 slices bacon, cut in half
    crosswise
2 (10¾-ounce) cans fiesta
    Cheddar cheese soup

⅔ cup milk
¼ teaspoon pepper
12 ounces sliced ham or
    smoked turkey, chopped
6 tomato slices

•You can substitute an equal amount of macaroni for penne in this casserole, if you'd prefer.

Cook pasta according to package directions; drain.

Place bacon on a microwave-safe rack in a baking dish. Cover with paper towels. Microwave at HIGH 5 to 6 minutes or until crisp. Drain.

Combine soup, milk, and pepper; stir well. Add ham and pasta; stir well. Spoon mixture into a lightly greased 11- x 7- x 1½-inch baking dish. Top with tomato slices. Cover and bake at 350° for 30 minutes. Arrange bacon slices over tomato; cover and bake 10 more minutes or until hot. Yield: 6 servings.

Crunch-Coated Lemon Chicken

PREP: 11 MINUTES   COOK: 9 MINUTES

4 skinned and boned chicken
    breast halves
1 large egg, lightly beaten
¼ teaspoon salt
⅛ teaspoon ground red
    pepper

½ cup wheat germ
1 tablespoon butter or
    margarine
Vegetable cooking spray
3 tablespoons lemon juice
Garnish: lemon slices

•Use fine, dry bread-crumbs from a can to coat the chicken if you don't have wheat germ.

Place chicken between two sheets of heavy-duty plastic wrap, and flatten to ½-inch thickness, using a meat mallet or rolling pin.

Combine egg, salt, and pepper. Dip each piece of chicken in egg mixture, and dredge in wheat germ.

Melt butter in a large skillet coated with cooking spray over medium heat. Add chicken; cook 3 minutes on each side or until done. Remove chicken, and keep warm. Add lemon juice to skillet. Cook over high heat, deglazing skillet by scraping bits that cling to bottom; pour over chicken. Garnish, if desired. Yield: 4 servings.

Toasted Almond Chicken

PREP: 10 MINUTES   **COOK: 16 MINUTES**

•This almond-topped chicken is bathed in a rich, velvety cream sauce with a hint of sweet orange marmalade. Serve it over toast points or rice.

6 skinned and boned chicken breast halves
⅛ teaspoon salt
⅛ teaspoon black pepper
3 tablespoons butter or margarine, divided
1½ cups whipping cream

2 tablespoons orange marmalade
1 tablespoon Dijon mustard
⅛ teaspoon ground red pepper
1 (2.25-ounce) package sliced almonds, toasted

Place chicken between two sheets of heavy-duty plastic wrap, and flatten to ¼-inch thickness, using a meat mallet or rolling pin. Sprinkle with salt and black pepper.

Melt 1½ tablespoons butter in a large skillet over medium-high heat. Add half of chicken, and cook 2 minutes on each side or until golden. Remove chicken from skillet. Repeat procedure with remaining butter and chicken.

Reduce heat to medium; add whipping cream and next 3 ingredients to skillet, stirring well. Add chicken; sprinkle with almonds, and cook 8 minutes or until sauce thickens. Yield: 6 servings.

Chicken Fricassee

PREP: 13 MINUTES   **COOK: 20 MINUTES**

•Fricassee is a thick, chunky, stewlike dinner of browned chicken simmered with vegetables.

¼ cup butter or margarine, divided
6 skinned and boned chicken breast halves
¼ cup all-purpose flour
2 cups sliced fresh mushrooms
3 carrots, scraped and sliced

1 (1.1-ounce) envelope herb-with-lemon soup mix
1 cup half-and-half
½ cup water or white wine
2 teaspoons chicken bouillon granules

Melt 2 tablespoons butter in a large skillet over medium heat. Dredge chicken in flour; brown in butter. Remove from skillet; set aside.

Melt remaining 2 tablespoons butter in skillet; add mushrooms and carrot, and cook, stirring constantly, over medium heat 4 minutes or until tender.

Combine soup mix and remaining 3 ingredients; pour over mushroom mixture. Bring to a boil, stirring constantly. Add chicken; reduce heat, and simmer 10 minutes or until chicken is done. Yield: 6 servings.

TOASTED ALMOND CHICKEN

Paprika Chicken

PREP: 7 MINUTES   COOK: 14 MINUTES

1 tablespoon butter or
   margarine
4 skinned and boned chicken
   breast halves
1 (10¾-ounce) can cream of
   mushroom soup, undiluted
1 tablespoon paprika

½ teaspoon dried tarragon
½ teaspoon salt
½ teaspoon ground red
   pepper
⅓ cup sour cream
Hot cooked egg noodles
Chopped fresh parsley

Melt butter in a large nonstick skillet over medium-high heat; add chicken, and cook until browned on both sides.

Combine soup and next 4 ingredients, stirring well; add to skillet, turning chicken to coat. Cover and cook over medium heat 8 minutes or until chicken is done. Remove chicken; keep warm. Stir sour cream into pan drippings; cook, stirring constantly, 1 minute.

Arrange chicken over pasta; top with sour cream mixture. Sprinkle with parsley. Yield: 4 servings.

Garlic Chicken

PREP: 2 MINUTES   COOK: 18 MINUTES

•Mince fresh garlic for optimum flavor here. The simpler the recipe, the bigger difference it makes to use fresh ingredients.

4 skinned and boned chicken
   breast halves
½ cup all-purpose flour
¼ cup butter or margarine
4 large cloves garlic, minced
   (2 tablespoons)

1 cup apple juice
2 tablespoons lemon juice
½ teaspoon pepper

Dredge chicken in flour. Melt butter in a large skillet over medium heat; add chicken and garlic. Cook 4 to 5 minutes on each side or until chicken is done. Remove chicken from skillet; keep warm.

Add apple juice, lemon juice, and pepper to skillet; bring mixture to a boil. Boil, uncovered, 4 minutes or until reduced to ½ cup. Pour sauce over chicken, and serve immediately. Yield: 4 servings.

Lemon Chicken with Snow Peas

PREP: 25 MINUTES   COOK: 15 MINUTES

3 (3-ounce) packages chicken
   ramen noodle soup mix*
4 skinned and boned chicken
   breast halves
½ cup all-purpose flour
½ teaspoon salt
¼ teaspoon pepper

½ cup lemon juice, divided
3 tablespoons vegetable oil
1 clove garlic, crushed
½ pound fresh or 1 (10-
   ounce) package frozen
   snow pea pods, trimmed

Cook soup according to package directions; drain noodles, reserving 1½ cups broth. Keep noodles warm.

Place chicken between two sheets of heavy-duty plastic wrap, and pound to ¼-inch thickness, using a meat mallet or rolling pin.

Combine flour, salt, and pepper in a shallow dish. Dip chicken in ¼ cup lemon juice, and dredge in flour mixture.

Heat oil in a large nonstick skillet over medium-high heat; add chicken. Cook 3 to 4 minutes or until chicken is browned on both sides. Reduce heat to medium, and add remaining ¼ cup lemon juice, reserved broth, garlic, and snow peas. Simmer 4 to 5 minutes or until chicken is done and snow peas are crisp-tender. Serve immediately over hot cooked noodles. Yield: 4 servings.

*For soup mix, we used Campbell's.

NACHO CHICKEN

Nacho Chicken

PREP: 5 MINUTES   COOK: 25 MINUTES

•Nacho Doritos lend a crispy coating to this simple chicken recipe.

2 tablespoons mayonnaise
¼ teaspoon salt
¼ teaspoon dried Italian
     seasoning
2 skinned and boned chicken
     breast halves

¾ cup crushed nacho
     cheese-flavored tortilla
     chips (about 30)
1 tablespoon butter or
     margarine, melted

Combine first 3 ingredients; spread on both sides of chicken. Dredge chicken in crushed chips. Place chicken on a lightly greased baking sheet or jellyroll pan. Drizzle with butter. Bake at 350° for 20 to 25 minutes or until chicken is done. Yield: 2 servings.

Chicken Parmigiana

PREP: 12 MINUTES   COOK: 24 MINUTES

4 skinned and boned chicken
  breast halves
½ cup Italian-seasoned
  breadcrumbs
½ cup grated Parmesan
  cheese
1 large egg, lightly beaten

2 tablespoons butter or
  margarine
1 (14-ounce) jar spaghetti
  sauce (about 2 cups)
1 cup (4 ounces) shredded
  mozzarella cheese

•Use your favorite brand
of spaghetti sauce—the
spicier the better—in this
recipe.

Place chicken between two sheets of heavy-duty plastic wrap, and
flatten to ¼-inch thickness, using a meat mallet or rolling pin.

Combine breadcrumbs and Parmesan cheese. Dip chicken in beaten
egg; dredge in breadcrumb mixture.

Melt butter in a large skillet; add chicken, and brown on each side over
medium-high heat. Arrange chicken in a lightly greased 11- x 7- x 1½-
inch baking dish. Pour spaghetti sauce over chicken, and sprinkle with
mozzarella cheese. Cover and bake at 375° for 20 minutes or until thoroughly heated. Yield: 4 servings.

Chicken in Mustard Cream Sauce

PREP: 5 MINUTES   COOK: 12 MINUTES

4 skinned and boned chicken
  breast halves
⅛ teaspoon pepper
1 tablespoon Dijon mustard
2 tablespoons olive oil
¼ cup whipping cream

¼ cup dry white wine
2 teaspoons Dijon mustard
1 teaspoon green peppercorns
  packed in vinegar
  (optional)

Place chicken between two sheets of heavy-duty plastic wrap, and
flatten to ¼-inch thickness, using a meat mallet or rolling pin.
Sprinkle chicken with pepper. Coat 1 side of chicken breast halves
evenly with 1 tablespoon mustard.

Cook chicken in oil in a large skillet over medium heat 5 minutes on
each side or until chicken is done. Remove chicken from skillet; set aside,
and keep warm (reserve drippings in skillet).

Add whipping cream, wine, 2 teaspoons mustard, and, if desired,
peppercorns to skillet; cook, stirring constantly, until mixture thickens.
Spoon sauce over chicken. Yield: 4 servings.

Chicken with Lime Butter

PREP: 4 MINUTES   COOK: 21 MINUTES

•The lime butter in this recipe is also good spooned over grilled fish or steamed vegetables.

3 tablespoons all-purpose
   flour
1 teaspoon salt
½ teaspoon pepper
6 skinned and boned chicken
   breast halves
⅓ cup vegetable oil

¼ cup fresh lime juice (about
   2 limes)
½ cup butter or margarine,
   cut up
1 tablespoon minced fresh
   chives
½ teaspoon dried tarragon

Combine first 3 ingredients. Dredge chicken in flour mixture. Brown chicken in hot oil in a large skillet over medium-high heat. Cover, reduce heat, and cook 10 minutes or until chicken is done. Remove chicken from skillet, and set aside. Drain pan drippings from skillet.

  Pour lime juice into skillet. Cook over medium heat just until bubbly. Add butter, chives, and tarragon to skillet. Cook, stirring constantly, until butter melts and mixture thickens slightly. Remove lime butter from heat, and spoon over chicken. Yield: 6 servings.

Oregano Chicken

PREP: 5 MINUTES   COOK: 40 MINUTES

•The herbed cooking liquid simmers into a flavorful *au jus* for rice or bread.

¼ cup butter or margarine,
   melted
¼ cup lemon juice
2 tablespoons Worcestershire
   sauce
2 tablespoons soy sauce

1½ teaspoons dried oregano
1 large clove garlic, crushed
6 skinned and boned chicken
   breast halves
Hot cooked rice

Combine first 6 ingredients; stir well. Place chicken in an ungreased 13- x 9- x 2-inch baking dish. Pour butter mixture over chicken. Cover and bake at 375° for 30 minutes. Uncover and bake 10 more minutes. Transfer chicken to a serving platter. Serve chicken and, if desired, juices over rice. Yield: 6 servings.

Pepper-Jack Chicken

PREP: 32 MINUTES   COOK: 15 MINUTES

¼ cup mayonnaise, divided
¾ cup (3 ounces) shredded
    Monterey Jack cheese
    with peppers
2 tablespoons chopped fresh
    cilantro

3 tablespoons sour cream
1 tablespoon finely chopped
    pickled jalapeño peppers
1 clove garlic, minced
6 skinned and boned chicken
    breast halves

Combine 3 tablespoons mayonnaise, cheese, and next 4 ingredients, stirring well. Set aside.

Place chicken between two sheets of heavy-duty plastic wrap, and flatten to ¼-inch thickness, using a meat mallet or rolling pin. Brush both sides of chicken lightly with remaining 1 tablespoon mayonnaise; place chicken on rack in a broiler pan.

Broil 5½ inches from heat (with electric oven door partially opened) 5 minutes on each side. Spread cheese mixture evenly over chicken; broil 5 more minutes or until mixture is browned. Yield: 6 servings.

Skillet Chicken Olé

PREP: 6 MINUTES   COOK: 27 MINUTES

4 skinned and boned chicken
    breast halves, cubed
4 cloves garlic, crushed
1 small onion, chopped
2 tablespoons olive oil
1 (10-ounce) can diced
    tomatoes and green chiles,
    undrained
1 (10-ounce) package frozen
    whole kernel corn

1 (2¼-ounce) can sliced ripe
    olives, drained
½ teaspoon salt
½ teaspoon pepper
1 cup (4 ounces) shredded
    Cheddar cheese
Hot cooked rice

Cook first 3 ingredients in hot oil in a large skillet over medium-high heat, stirring constantly, 5 minutes. Add tomatoes and green chiles and next 4 ingredients. Bring to a boil; cover, reduce heat, and simmer 10 minutes. Uncover and simmer 10 more minutes. Sprinkle with cheese, and serve over rice. Yield: 4 servings.

Paella

PREP: **7** MINUTES   COOK: **45** MINUTES

•Paella is a Spanish one-dish meal. We simplified it by using packaged chicken strips and other convenience products.

1½ pounds chicken breast strips (tenders)
2 tablespoons olive oil
2 cloves garlic, crushed
1 large onion, finely chopped
2 (14½-ounce) cans stewed tomatoes, undrained
1 (10-ounce) package saffron rice, uncooked

1 cup water
½ teaspoon dried oregano
½ teaspoon ground cumin
1 (16-ounce) package peeled frozen cooked shrimp
1 (10-ounce) package frozen English peas
1 (6½-ounce) can minced clams, drained

Brown chicken in oil in a Dutch oven over medium heat. Add garlic and onion. Cook, stirring constantly, 5 minutes or until chicken is done. Stir in tomatoes and next 4 ingredients. Bring to a boil; cover, reduce heat, and simmer 25 minutes. Add frozen shrimp, peas, and clams; cover and simmer 10 more minutes. Serve immediately. Yield: 6 servings.

Chicken and Snow Pea Stir-Fry

PREP: **18** MINUTES   COOK: **8** MINUTES

¾ cup chicken broth
¼ cup soy sauce
1½ teaspoons cornstarch
1 tablespoon vegetable or peanut oil
2 skinned and boned chicken breast halves, cut into thin strips
1½ cups sliced celery

¼ pound fresh snow pea pods, trimmed
4 large fresh mushrooms, sliced
3 green onions, sliced
½ cup slivered almonds, toasted
Hot cooked rice

Combine first 3 ingredients in a small bowl; set aside.

Pour oil around top of a preheated wok, coating sides, or in a large nonstick skillet; heat briefly at medium-high (375°). Add chicken; cook, stirring constantly, 4 minutes or until chicken is almost done.

Add celery and next 3 ingredients; cook, stirring constantly, 3 to 4 minutes or until vegetables are tender and chicken is done. Stir in almonds.

Add broth mixture; cook, stirring gently, until mixture thickens and boils. Boil 1 minute, stirring gently. Serve over rice. Yield: 3 servings.

PAELLA

Browned Butter and Chicken Fettuccine

PREP: 7 MINUTES   COOK: 10 MINUTES

12 ounces dried fettuccine,
    uncooked
½ cup butter
4 skinned and boned chicken
    breast halves, cut into
    strips
1 clove garlic, crushed
1 (2.25-ounce) package
    slivered almonds, toasted

½ cup chopped fresh parsley
2 tablespoons dry white wine
1 teaspoon lemon juice
½ teaspoon salt
¼ cup freshly grated
    Parmesan cheese

•Margarine is no substitute
when it comes to browning
butter for this simple dish.
The high quality and flavor
of real butter are necessary
for best results.

Cook pasta according to package directions; drain and keep warm.

  Meanwhile, melt butter in a large skillet over medium-high heat,
swirling skillet until butter is browned. Add chicken, garlic, and
almonds; cook 4 minutes or until chicken is done. Stir in parsley and
next 3 ingredients; toss with hot cooked pasta. Sprinkle with cheese,
and serve immediately. Yield: 4 servings.

Chinese Red Pepper Chicken

PREP: 11 MINUTES   **CHILL: 30 MINUTES**

COOK: 14 MINUTES

•Chow mein noodles provide a crunchy base here. Rice works fine, too, if it's on hand.

2 skinned and boned chicken breast halves, cut into thin strips
1 teaspoon grated fresh ginger or ¼ teaspoon ground ginger
2 cloves garlic, minced
2 tablespoons peanut oil, divided
1 medium-size sweet red pepper, seeded and cut into thin strips

1 medium onion, cut into thin strips
1 cup broccoli flowerets
1 cup chicken broth
1 tablespoon cornstarch
2 tablespoons plum sauce
1 tablespoon Worcestershire sauce
1 tablespoon soy sauce
Chow mein noodles

Combine first 3 ingredients, stirring to coat chicken; cover and chill 30 minutes.

Heat 1 tablespoon oil in a large nonstick skillet over medium heat. Add chicken, and stir-fry 5 to 7 minutes or until done; remove chicken.

Heat remaining tablespoon oil in skillet over medium-high heat. Add pepper strips, onion, and broccoli; stir-fry 2 to 4 minutes or until crisp-tender. Remove vegetables from skillet.

Combine broth and next 4 ingredients, stirring until smooth. Add broth mixture to skillet; cook over medium heat, stirring constantly, until thickened and bubbly. Return chicken and vegetables to skillet, and cook until thoroughly heated. Serve over chow mein noodles. Yield: 2 servings.

Chicken-Almond Stir-Fry

PREP: 6 MINUTES   **COOK: 10 MINUTES**

2 tablespoons vegetable or
   sesame oil
4 skinned and boned chicken
   breast halves, cut into thin
   strips
1 (2.25-ounce) package sliced
   almonds
1 (16-ounce) package frozen
   broccoli, carrots, and
   water chestnuts

1 tablespoon cornstarch
1 tablespoon brown sugar
½ teaspoon ground ginger
½ cup soy sauce
⅓ cup pineapple juice
Hot cooked rice

Pour oil around top of a preheated wok, coating sides, or in a large
nonstick skillet. Heat briefly at medium-high (375°). Add chicken
and almonds; stir-fry 2 minutes. Add frozen vegetables; cover and
cook 4 minutes, stirring once.

Combine cornstarch and next 4 ingredients; add to wok. Cook, stirring
constantly, 2 to 3 minutes or until mixture thickens. Serve over rice.
Yield: 4 servings.

Quick Chicken and Rice Cacciatore

PREP: 8 MINUTES   COOK: 20 MINUTES

•Cacciatore means prepared "hunter-style" with onions and herbs; commercial spaghetti sauce makes it easy.

4 skinned and boned chicken breast halves, cut into 1-inch pieces
½ cup chopped onion
2 tablespoons vegetable oil
2 cups spaghetti sauce
1½ cups water

1 green pepper, seeded and cut into strips
½ teaspoon dried oregano
½ teaspoon dried basil
1½ cups instant rice, uncooked

Cook chicken and onion in oil in a large skillet until lightly browned, stirring often. Add spaghetti sauce and next 4 ingredients; stir well. Bring mixture to a boil; stir in rice. Cover, remove from heat, and let stand 5 minutes or until liquid is absorbed and rice is tender. Yield: 4 servings.

Chicken-Rice Florentine

PREP: 5 MINUTES   COOK: 23 MINUTES

4 slices bacon
6 skinned and boned chicken breast halves, cut into 1-inch pieces
1 medium onion, chopped
¾ cup water
½ teaspoon salt
1 (10½-ounce) can chicken broth, undiluted

1 (10-ounce) package frozen chopped spinach, thawed and drained
1 (8-ounce) can sliced water chestnuts, drained
2 cups instant rice, uncooked
½ cup (2 ounces) freshly grated Parmesan cheese

Cook bacon in a large skillet or saucepan over medium heat until crisp; drain, reserving 1 tablespoon drippings in skillet. Crumble bacon, and set aside.

Add chicken and onion to reserved drippings; cook over medium heat, stirring constantly, until chicken is done. Add ¾ cup water and next 4 ingredients. Bring to a boil; stir in rice. Cover, remove from heat, and let stand 5 minutes or until liquid is absorbed and rice is tender. Stir in bacon and cheese. Yield: 6 servings.

Baked Chicken Nuggets

PREP: 16 MINUTES   COOK: 20 MINUTES

½ cup fine, dry breadcrumbs
¼ cup grated Parmesan
   cheese
½ teaspoon dried basil
½ teaspoon dried thyme
¼ teaspoon salt

4 skinned and boned chicken
   breast halves, cut into
   1-inch pieces
¼ cup butter or margarine,
   melted

•Kids will gobble these up, especially with a squirt of ketchup.

Combine first 5 ingredients in a heavy-duty, zip-top plastic bag; seal bag, and shake well. Dip chicken in butter, and shake, a few pieces at a time, in breadcrumb mixture. Place chicken on a greased baking sheet. Bake at 400° for 20 minutes or until browned. Yield: 4 servings.

Honey-Ginger Chicken Kabobs

PREP: 24 MINUTES   GRILL: 12 MINUTES

1½ pounds skinned and boned
   chicken breast halves, cut
   into 1-inch pieces
¼ teaspoon salt
¼ teaspoon pepper
1 sweet yellow pepper, seeded
   and cut into 1-inch pieces
1 sweet red pepper, seeded
   and cut into 1-inch pieces

1 (15-ounce) can or jar baby
   corn, drained and cut in
   half
⅓ cup hoisin sauce
⅓ cup honey
½ teaspoon minced fresh
   ginger or ⅛ teaspoon
   ground ginger
1 clove garlic, crushed

Sprinkle chicken with salt and pepper. Thread chicken, pepper pieces, and corn onto eight long metal skewers.

Combine hoisin sauce and remaining 3 ingredients, stirring well. Brush lightly on kabobs. Grill kabobs, covered with grill lid, over medium-hot coals (350° to 400°) 12 minutes, turning and basting with hoisin sauce mixture. Yield: 4 servings.

Creamy Chicken Divan

PREP: 3 MINUTES   COOK: 15 MINUTES

2 (10-ounce) packages frozen broccoli spears
1 (10¾-ounce) can cream of chicken soup, undiluted
3 cups chopped cooked chicken
¼ teaspoon poultry seasoning
1 (8-ounce) carton sour cream
1 cup (4 ounces) shredded Cheddar cheese, divided
16 round buttery crackers, crushed (¾ cup)
2 tablespoons slivered almonds
1½ tablespoons butter or margarine, melted

Place broccoli in a shallow 2-quart baking dish. Cover tightly with heavy-duty plastic wrap; fold back a small corner of wrap to allow steam to escape. Microwave at HIGH 4 minutes; drain and set aside.

Combine soup, chicken, and poultry seasoning in a microwave-safe bowl; cover and microwave at HIGH 3 minutes. Stir in sour cream and ½ cup shredded cheese. Microwave, uncovered, at HIGH 2 minutes. Spoon chicken mixture over broccoli; sprinkle with remaining cheese.

Combine cracker crumbs, almonds, and butter; sprinkle over cheese. Microwave, uncovered, at HIGH 6 minutes. Yield: 6 servings.

Quick Chicken à la King

PREP: 4 MINUTES   COOK: 10 MINUTES

•Here's an easy entrée for two. Use any kind of bread you have on hand for toast.

1 cup chopped cooked chicken
¼ cup milk
¼ cup frozen English peas, thawed
½ teaspoon salt
¼ teaspoon pepper
1 (10¾-ounce) can cream of chicken soup, undiluted
1 (4-ounce) can sliced mushrooms, drained
1 (2-ounce) jar diced pimiento, drained
4 slices whole wheat or other bread, toasted
Paprika

Combine first 8 ingredients in a large saucepan; cook over low heat 10 minutes, stirring often.

Cut each slice of toast in half, if desired. Spoon chicken mixture over toast on two plates. Sprinkle with paprika. Yield: 2 servings.

CREAMED CHICKEN AND BISCUITS

Creamed Chicken and Biscuits

PREP: 5 MINUTES   COOK: 15 MINUTES

2 cups chopped cooked chicken
½ cup milk
½ teaspoon poultry seasoning
¼ teaspoon pepper
1 (10¾-ounce) can cream of
    chicken soup, undiluted

1 (10-ounce) package frozen
    mixed vegetables
1 (5.5- or 6-ounce) can
    refrigerated buttermilk
    biscuits

•You'll have one leftover
biscuit (for snacking) when
preparing this recipe.

•You can also serve the
chicken mixture over cornbread or waffles.

Combine first 6 ingredients in a saucepan. Cook over medium heat
10 to 15 minutes or until thoroughly heated, stirring often.

Meanwhile, bake biscuits according to package directions.

Split hot biscuits in half; spoon chicken mixture over biscuit halves.
Yield: 4 servings.

Ramen Egg Foo Yong

PREP: 19 MINUTES   COOK: 17 MINUTES

2 (3-ounce) packages chicken
   ramen noodle soup mix
6 large eggs
2 cups finely chopped cooked
   chicken
½ cup sliced green onions
½ teaspoon salt
½ teaspoon pepper
2 cloves garlic, crushed

1 (8-ounce) can sliced water
   chestnuts, drained and
   finely chopped
Vegetable cooking spray
2 tablespoons vegetable oil
2 tablespoons all-purpose
   flour
2 tablespoons soy sauce

Cook soup according to package directions; drain noodles, reserving broth. Set aside.

Beat eggs in a large bowl until blended. Stir in noodles, chicken, and next 5 ingredients.

Coat a large nonstick skillet with cooking spray; place over medium-high heat until hot. For each patty, carefully pour about ½ cup noodle mixture into skillet. Cook until eggs are set and patties are lightly browned. Remove to a hot ovenproof platter; keep warm. Repeat procedure with remaining noodle mixture.

Whisk together oil, flour, and soy sauce in skillet; gradually whisk in reserved broth. Cook, stirring constantly, 2 to 3 minutes or until mixture is thickened. Serve over patties. Yield: 6 servings.

Turkey Pie

PREP: 12 MINUTES   COOK: 45 MINUTES

•Cover this savory pie loosely with foil near the end of cooking if the crust starts to get too brown.

½ (15-ounce) package
   refrigerated piecrusts
3 large eggs, lightly beaten
1 cup (4 ounces) shredded
   sharp Cheddar cheese,
   divided
2 cups chopped cooked turkey
⅓ cup chopped onion

⅓ cup chicken broth
¼ cup half and half
¼ cup mayonnaise
2 tablespoons all-purpose flour
¼ teaspoon salt
¼ teaspoon pepper
3 drops hot sauce
1 (8-ounce) carton sour cream

Fit piecrust into a 9-inch pieplate according to package directions; fold edges under, and crimp. Prick bottom and sides lightly with a fork. Bake at 400° for 10 minutes.

Combine eggs, ½ cup cheese, and remaining 10 ingredients in a large bowl, stirring until blended; pour into prepared crust. Bake, uncovered, at 400° for 20 minutes. Reduce oven temperature to 350°. Bake 10 to 15 more minutes or until set; sprinkle with remaining ½ cup cheese for last 2 minutes of baking. Yield: 6 servings.

Turkey Tacos

PREP: **4** MINUTES   COOK: **12** MINUTES

8 taco shells
1¼ pounds ground turkey
¾ cup frozen chopped onion
½ cup chopped sweet red or
    green pepper
1 jalapeño pepper, seeded and
    chopped
1 tablespoon vegetable oil
1 (1-ounce) envelope onion
    soup mix

1 (1¼-ounce) package taco
    seasoning mix
¾ cup water
1 cup chunky salsa
Toppings: shredded Cheddar
    cheese, sour cream,
    shredded lettuce

Heat taco shells according to package directions.

  Meanwhile, cook turkey and next 3 ingredients in hot oil in a large non-stick skillet over medium-high heat, stirring constantly, until turkey is browned, stirring until it crumbles. Add soup mix, taco seasoning mix, and water. Cover and cook 5 minutes; uncover and simmer 2 minutes. Stir in salsa, and cook until thoroughly heated.

  Fill each taco shell with ½ cup turkey mixture, and top with desired toppings. Serve immediately. Yield: 8 servings.

CATFISH MEUNIÈRE

Catfish Meunière

PREP: 8 MINUTES COOK: 8 MINUTES

1 large egg, lightly beaten
¼ cup milk
½ cup all-purpose flour
½ teaspoon salt
½ teaspoon ground red
    pepper
4 farm-raised catfish fillets
½ cup butter or margarine,
    divided

¼ cup vegetable oil
2 tablespoons chopped fresh
    parsley
2 tablespoons lemon juice
½ teaspoon Worcestershire
    sauce
Garnishes: fresh parsley
    sprigs, lemon wedges

•*Meunière* is a French term for fish that's lightly seasoned, dusted with flour, and pan-fried.

Combine egg and milk in a large shallow bowl. Combine flour, salt, and pepper in a shallow dish. Dip fish in egg mixture, and dredge in flour mixture.

Melt ¼ cup butter in a large nonstick skillet over medium heat. Add oil; increase heat to medium-high. Place fish in skillet, and cook 4 minutes on each side or until fish flakes easily when tested with a fork. Drain on paper towels.

Melt remaining ¼ cup butter in skillet; stir in chopped parsley, lemon juice, and Worcestershire sauce. Spoon over fish. Garnish, if desired. Yield: 4 servings.

Crunchy Potato Fish Fry

PREP: 5 MINUTES COOK: 12 MINUTES

1 (2-ounce) envelope instant
    mashed potato granules
2 tablespoons sesame seeds
1 large egg, lightly beaten
1 tablespoon lemon juice
1 teaspoon salt

⅛ teaspoon pepper
1 (24-ounce) package or 2
    (12-ounce) packages
    frozen fish fillets, thawed
¼ cup vegetable oil, divided

•Look for frozen fish fillets in your grocer's freezer section. Whiting, pollock, ocean perch, and cod each come packaged in frozen blocks.

Combine potato granules and sesame seeds in a large shallow dish. Combine egg and next 3 ingredients. Dip fish in egg mixture; dredge in potato mixture.

Heat 2 tablespoons oil in a large skillet over medium-high heat; fry half of fish in oil 3 minutes on each side or until golden. Drain fish on paper towels. Repeat procedure with remaining oil and fish. Yield: 6 servings.

Lemon-Coated Fillets

PREP: 4 MINUTES   COOK: 6 MINUTES

¼ cup butter or margarine	¼ teaspoon salt
2 teaspoons lemon juice	¼ teaspoon pepper
4 small orange roughy or other firm-fleshed fish fillets (about 1½ pounds)	¾ cup Italian-seasoned breadcrumbs
	Paprika

Place butter in a 1-cup glass measuring cup; microwave at HIGH 30 seconds or until melted. Stir in lemon juice.

Sprinkle fillets with salt and pepper. Brush both sides with butter mixture, and dredge in breadcrumbs. Arrange fish in an 11- x 7- x 1½-inch baking dish. Sprinkle with paprika. Cover with wax paper. Microwave at HIGH 5 minutes or until fish flakes easily when tested with a fork. Yield: 4 servings.

Skillet Fish in Caper Sauce

PREP: 3 MINUTES   COOK: 20 MINUTES

•A pancake turner or flat spatula is the ideal tool for transferring and serving delicate fish.

1 medium onion, chopped	2 tablespoons capers
1 tablespoon olive oil	1 teaspoon dried oregano
2 (14½-ounce) cans or 1 (28-ounce) can Italian stewed tomatoes, undrained	1 teaspoon dried basil
	¼ teaspoon garlic powder
	2 pounds orange roughy fillets

Cook onion in oil in a large skillet over medium heat 5 minutes or until tender, stirring often. Add tomatoes and next 4 ingredients; cook 2 minutes. Remove mixture from skillet.

Add fillets to skillet; top with tomato mixture. Cover and cook over medium heat 10 to 12 minutes or until fish flakes easily when tested with a fork. Serve with a slotted spatula (so fish won't tear). Yield: 6 servings.

Salmon Bake with Pecan-Crunch Coating

PREP: 5 MINUTES   COOK: 15 MINUTES

4 salmon fillets (about 1½ inches thick)
¼ teaspoon salt
⅛ teaspoon pepper
2 tablespoons Dijon mustard
2 tablespoons butter or margarine, melted
1½ tablespoons honey
¼ cup soft breadcrumbs
¼ cup finely chopped pecans
1 tablespoon chopped fresh parsley
Garnish: lemon slices

• This pecan-crunch coating also works well on grouper or other white fillets.

Sprinkle salmon with salt and pepper; place, skin side down, in a lightly greased 11- x 7- x 1½-inch or 9-inch square baking dish.

Combine mustard, butter, and honey; brush over salmon. Combine breadcrumbs, pecans, and parsley; spoon evenly across top of salmon. Bake, uncovered, at 450° for 12 to 15 minutes or until fish flakes easily when tested with a fork. Garnish, if desired. Yield: 4 servings.

SALMON BAKE WITH
PECAN-CRUNCH COATING

Grouper with Pecan Sauce

PREP: 15 MINUTES   COOK: 15 MINUTES

4 (1-inch-thick) grouper or
   flounder fillets (1½ to 2
   pounds)
1 tablespoon soy sauce
¼ cup all-purpose flour
3 tablespoons vegetable oil

1 cup whipping cream
1 tablespoon dark corn syrup
   or molasses
1 teaspoon soy sauce
½ cup pecan pieces, toasted

Place fillets in a shallow baking dish. Brush with 1 tablespoon soy sauce; cover and chill 10 minutes.

  Dredge fish in flour, shaking off excess flour. Heat oil in a large nonstick skillet over medium-high heat until hot. Add fish; cook 6 to 8 minutes on each side or until browned and fish flakes easily when tested with a fork. Remove fish from skillet, and keep warm.

  Wipe skillet dry with a paper towel. Add whipping cream and corn syrup to skillet; bring to a boil over medium heat. Boil until mixture is reduced to ¾ cup (about 5 minutes). Stir in 1 teaspoon soy sauce and pecans; spoon sauce over fish. Yield: 4 servings.

Easy Crab Bake

PREP: 15 MINUTES   COOK: 30 MINUTES

1 large egg, lightly beaten
¾ cup mayonnaise
2 tablespoons lemon juice
1½ teaspoons hot sauce
¼ teaspoon salt
1 pound fresh crabmeat,
   drained and flaked

¼ cup fine, dry breadcrumbs
1 tablespoon butter or
   margarine, melted
Lemon wedges (optional)

Combine first 5 ingredients; stir well. Pick through crabmeat to remove any bits of shell and cartilage. Fold crabmeat into egg mixture. Spoon mixture into a lightly greased 1-quart baking dish.

  Combine breadcrumbs and butter; sprinkle over crabmeat mixture. Bake, uncovered, at 325° for 25 to 30 minutes. Serve with lemon wedges, if desired. Yield: 4 servings.

SCALLOPS IN VERMOUTH CREAM

Scallops in Vermouth Cream

PREP: 4 MINUTES   COOK: 10 MINUTES

1 pound sea scallops
2 tablespoons all-purpose
   flour
2 tablespoons butter or
   margarine

¼ cup dry vermouth or
   other white wine
½ cup whipping cream
¼ teaspoon salt
⅛ teaspoon pepper

- Vermouth is a white wine that has been flavored with herbs and spices.

- Drench crusty bread or rice in this rich vermouth cream.

- Sea scallops can be as large as three inches in diameter. Bay scallops are much smaller.

Toss scallops with flour. Melt butter in a large skillet over medium heat; add scallops. Cook 4 to 5 minutes or until scallops turn white throughout and are lightly browned on both sides, turning occasionally. Remove scallops from skillet.

 Add vermouth to skillet, stirring to loosen bits from bottom of skillet; bring to a boil. Cook 2 minutes or until vermouth is reduced by half. Stir in whipping cream, salt, and pepper; reduce heat to low. Add scallops; cook just until thoroughly heated. Yield: 2 servings.

SHRIMP CREOLE

Shrimp Creole

PREP: 8 MINUTES   COOK: 10 MINUTES

•Make this dish even quicker by using one 16-ounce package of frozen peeled cooked shrimp in place of fresh shrimp, and one cup of frozen seasoning blend instead of green pepper, celery, and green onions.

2 tablespoons butter or margarine
½ cup chopped green pepper
¼ cup chopped celery
4 green onions, thinly sliced
1 clove garlic, minced
1 (14½-ounce) can Cajun-style stewed tomatoes, undrained
1 (6-ounce) can tomato paste
½ cup water

2 teaspoons dried parsley flakes
½ teaspoon chicken bouillon granules
½ teaspoon salt
¼ teaspoon ground red pepper
1 pound peeled medium-size fresh shrimp (1⅓ pounds unpeeled)
Hot cooked rice

Melt butter in a large skillet over medium-high heat; add green pepper and next 3 ingredients. Cook, stirring constantly, 4 minutes. Add tomatoes and next 6 ingredients; cook 2 minutes over medium heat. Add shrimp, and cook 4 minutes or until shrimp turn pink. Serve over rice. Yield: 3 to 4 servings.

Garlic Scampi

8 ounces dried angel hair
    pasta, uncooked
½ cup butter or margarine
4 large cloves garlic, minced
1 pound peeled large fresh
    shrimp (1⅓ pounds
    unpeeled)

⅓ cup dry white wine
¼ teaspoon freshly ground
    pepper
¾ cup grated Parmesan or
    Romano cheese
¼ cup chopped fresh parsley

•Try this buttery sauced shrimp over French bread, rice, or egg noodles.

Cook pasta according to package directions; drain and place on a large serving platter.

    Meanwhile, melt butter in a large skillet over medium heat. Add garlic and shrimp; cook, stirring constantly, 3 to 5 minutes or until shrimp turn pink. Add wine and pepper. Bring to a boil; cook, stirring constantly, 30 seconds. Remove from heat; stir in cheese and parsley. Pour shrimp mixture over pasta. Toss gently. Serve immediately. Yield: 4 servings.

Artichoke and Shrimp Linguine

8 ounces dried linguine,
    uncooked
¼ cup olive oil
1 pound peeled medium-size
    fresh shrimp (1⅓ pounds
    unpeeled)
½ teaspoon dried crushed red
    pepper
3 cloves garlic, minced

1 (14-ounce) can quartered
    artichoke hearts, drained
1 (2¼-ounce) can sliced ripe
    olives, drained
¼ cup lemon juice
⅛ teaspoon salt
⅛ teaspoon pepper
½ cup grated Parmesan
    cheese

Cook pasta according to package directions; drain and keep warm in a large bowl.

    Meanwhile, heat oil in a large skillet over medium-high heat until hot; add shrimp, red pepper, and garlic. Cook, stirring constantly, 3 to 5 minutes or until shrimp turn pink. Stir in artichoke hearts and next 4 ingredients; cook just until thoroughly heated. Add artichoke mixture to pasta, and sprinkle with cheese. Yield: 4 servings.

Shrimp and Tomato Fettuccine

PREP: 6 MINUTES   COOK: 14 MINUTES

8 ounces dried fettuccine, uncooked

2 (14½-ounce) cans diced tomatoes, undrained

1 pound peeled medium-size fresh shrimp (1⅓ pounds unpeeled)

¼ cup olive oil

1 teaspoon dried basil

½ teaspoon freshly ground pepper

¼ teaspoon salt

3 cloves garlic, minced

1 shallot, minced, or ¼ cup minced onion

Freshly grated Romano or Parmesan cheese

Cook pasta according to package directions; drain and keep warm on a large serving platter.

   Meanwhile, drain diced tomato, reserving ¼ cup liquid. Cook shrimp, diced tomato, reserved liquid, oil, and next 5 ingredients in a large skillet 5 to 7 minutes or until shrimp turn pink. Spoon over pasta, and sprinkle with cheese. Serve immediately. Yield: 4 servings.

Shrimp and Red Pepper Pasta

PREP: 16 MINUTES   COOK: 15 MINUTES

¾ cup commercial Ranch-style dressing

1 (3-ounce) package refrigerated shredded Parmesan cheese

8 ounces dried angel hair pasta, uncooked

3 tablespoons butter or margarine

½ pound sliced fresh mushrooms

1 pound peeled medium-size fresh shrimp (1⅓ pounds unpeeled)

1 (12-ounce) jar roasted red peppers, drained and cut into strips

½ cup sliced fresh basil

¼ teaspoon pepper

Combine salad dressing and cheese; set aside. Cook pasta according to package directions; drain.

   Meanwhile, melt butter in a large skillet or Dutch oven over medium-high heat; add mushrooms. Cook, stirring constantly, 2 minutes. Add shrimp; cook 3 to 5 minutes or until shrimp turn pink, stirring often. Drain excess liquid.

SHRIMP AND RED PEPPER PASTA

Combine hot cooked pasta, salad dressing mixture, shrimp mixture, red pepper strips, basil, and pepper in a large bowl; toss gently. Serve immediately. Yield: 4 servings.

Shrimp Versailles

PREP: 10 MINUTES   COOK: 17 MINUTES

•This rich shrimp dish is also good spooned over garlic bread instead of pasta.

12 ounces dried angel hair pasta, uncooked
2 green onions, sliced
3 tablespoons butter or margarine, melted
1½ pounds peeled large fresh shrimp (2 pounds unpeeled)
1 (8-ounce) package cream cheese, cubed

¼ cup milk
½ cup (2 ounces) shredded Swiss cheese
¼ cup dry white wine
Dash of ground red pepper
¼ cup fine, dry breadcrumbs
2 tablespoons butter or margarine, melted

Cook pasta according to package directions; drain and keep warm.

Meanwhile, cook green onions in 3 tablespoons butter in a large skillet over medium heat until tender. Add shrimp. Cook over medium heat 5 minutes or until shrimp turn pink, stirring occasionally. Remove shrimp with a slotted spoon.

Add cream cheese and milk to skillet; cook over low heat, stirring constantly, until cheese melts. Stir in Swiss cheese and wine. Add shrimp and red pepper; cook, stirring constantly, just until heated. Pour shrimp mixture into a lightly greased 1½-quart casserole.

Combine breadcrumbs and 2 tablespoons butter; sprinkle over casserole. Broil 5½ inches from heat (with electric oven door partially opened) 3 to 5 minutes or until golden. Serve shrimp mixture over pasta. Yield: 6 servings.

Broccoli and Cheese Potatoes

PREP: 3 MINUTES   **COOK: 22 MINUTES**

1 (10-ounce) package frozen
  broccoli in cheese sauce
2 large baking potatoes (about
  1½ pounds)

4 ounces Mexican-flavored
  process cheese spread*
Chunky salsa (optional)

•This loaded spud makes a
great light supper.

Microwave broccoli according to package directions. Set aside.

Scrub potatoes; prick several times with a fork. Place potatoes 1 inch apart on a microwave-safe rack or paper towels. Microwave at HIGH 10 to 13 minutes, turning and rearranging once; let stand 2 minutes. Cut an X to within ½ inch of bottom of each potato. Squeeze potatoes from opposite sides and opposite ends to open; fluff pulp with a fork.

Place cheese spread in a bowl. Cover and microwave at HIGH 1 minute, stirring once. Add broccoli to cheese, and stir gently. Spoon broccoli mixture over potatoes. Top with salsa, if desired. Serve immediately. Yield: 2 servings.

*For cheese spread, we used Mexican-flavored Velveeta. Plain Velveeta tastes fine, too, in this recipe—the potatoes just aren't as spicy.

BROCCOLI AND CHEESE POTATO

TORTILLA PIE

Tortilla Pie

PREP: 11 MINUTES   COOK: 25 MINUTES

1 (16-ounce) can refried beans
1 teaspoon chili powder
½ teaspoon ground cumin
8 (8-inch) flour tortillas
1 cup chunky salsa, divided
2 (4- or 6-ounce) cartons
    guacamole

1 (8-ounce) package shredded
    Mexican cheese blend*
Garnishes: sour cream,
    additional salsa and
    guacamole

•This Mexican meatless entrée is a colorful stack that comes out of the pan intact. Add one cup shredded cooked chicken over the first layer of beans, if desired.

•Use a can of black beans, drained, instead of refried beans in the pie if you'd prefer. (See photo.)

Combine first 3 ingredients, stirring well.

  Place 1 tortilla in a lightly greased 9-inch round cakepan; spread with half of bean mixture, and top with another tortilla. Spread with ½ cup salsa, and top with another tortilla. Spread with half of guacamole, and top with another tortilla. Sprinkle with half of cheese, and top with another tortilla.

Repeat layers with remaining ingredients, except cheese. (Pan will be full.) Cover and bake at 350° for 20 minutes; uncover and sprinkle with remaining cheese. Bake, uncovered, 3 to 5 more minutes. Cut into wedges to serve. Garnish, if desired. Yield: 6 servings.

*For cheese blend, we used Sargento.

Black Bean Chili Potatoes

PREP: 6 MINUTES   COOK: 30 MINUTES

4 large baking potatoes (about 3 pounds)
Vegetable cooking spray
1 tablespoon vegetable oil
3 cloves garlic, crushed
1 medium onion, chopped
1 (14½-ounce) can chili-style chunky tomatoes, undrained

1 (15-ounce) can black beans, drained
1 teaspoon chili powder
½ teaspoon ground cumin
4 green onions, sliced
1 cup (4 ounces) shredded Cheddar cheese
Sour cream (optional)

Scrub potatoes; prick each potato several times with a fork. Arrange potatoes 1 inch apart on a microwave-safe rack or on paper towels. Microwave at HIGH 22 to 24 minutes, turning and rearranging after 10 minutes. Let stand 2 minutes.

Meanwhile, coat a large saucepan or skillet with cooking spray; add oil. Place over medium-high heat until hot. Add garlic and onion; cook, stirring constantly, until tender. Stir in tomatoes and next 3 ingredients; cook over medium heat just until thoroughly heated, stirring occasionally. Remove from heat, and stir in green onions.

Cut an X to within ½ inch of bottom of each baked potato. Squeeze potatoes from opposite ends to open; fluff pulp with a fork. Spoon bean mixture over potatoes, and sprinkle with cheese. Top each potato with sour cream, if desired, and serve immediately. Yield: 4 servings.

Cheese Enchiladas

PREP: 14 MINUTES   **COOK: 35 MINUTES**

2 (10-ounce) cans enchilada
   sauce
1 (12-ounce) container cottage
   cheese
1 (8-ounce) carton sour cream
1 (4.5-ounce) can chopped
   green chiles, undrained
¼ teaspoon salt
8 (8-inch) flour tortillas

1 cup (4 ounces) shredded
   Monterey Jack cheese
   with peppers
1 (2¼-ounce) can sliced ripe
   olives, drained
1 cup (4 ounces) shredded
   Cheddar cheese
Garnishes: sour cream, sliced
   ripe olives, cilantro sprigs

Spread ¾ cup enchilada sauce in a lightly greased 13- x 9- x 2-inch baking dish.

Combine cottage cheese and next 3 ingredients; spoon about ⅓ cup mixture down center of each tortilla. Sprinkle evenly with Monterey Jack cheese; roll up, and place, seam side down, in baking dish. Top with remaining enchilada sauce; sprinkle with 1 can olives.

Cover and bake at 350° for 30 minutes. Uncover and sprinkle with Cheddar cheese. Bake 5 more minutes. Garnish, if desired. Serve immediately. Yield: 4 servings.

Southwestern Veggie Pizza

PREP: 8 MINUTES   **COOK: 20 MINUTES**

1 (16-ounce) Italian bread
   shell*
2 carrots, scraped and
   shredded, or ½ cup
   packaged shredded carrot
1 zucchini, sliced
1 clove garlic, minced

1 tablespoon olive oil
1 (11.5-ounce) jar black bean
   dip
½ cup chunky salsa
1 cup (4 ounces) shredded
   Monterey Jack cheese
   with peppers

Bake bread shell on a baking sheet at 350° for 5 minutes. Meanwhile, cook carrot, zucchini, and garlic in oil in a skillet over medium heat, stirring constantly, 3 to 5 minutes or until crisp-tender. Spread bean dip over bread shell; top with salsa and vegetables. Sprinkle with cheese. Bake at 350° for 10 minutes or until cheese melts. Yield: 3 to 4 servings.

*For the bread shell, we used a Boboli crust.

PAGE 116

PAGE 136

Salads, Soups & Sandwiches

PAGE 129

PAGE 120

LOOKING FOR A SIMPLE SUPPER? THIS COLLECTION OFFERS HEARTY CHOICES SUBSTANTIAL ENOUGH TO BE ONE-DISH MEALS, AS WELL AS LIGHTER FARE FOR SERVING ON THE SIDE.

PAGE 139

PAGE 110

Cantaloupe Salad

PREP: 10 MINUTES

•It's easy to use small amounts of frozen orange juice concentrate and leave the rest frozen. Just scoop the desired amount of slushy concentrate off the top, replace the lid, and return the remainder to the freezer.

½ cup mayonnaise
3 tablespoons frozen orange juice concentrate, thawed and undiluted

1 small cantaloupe, chilled
Leaf lettuce
1⅓ cups seedless green or red grapes

Combine mayonnaise and orange juice concentrate, stirring well.
Cut cantaloupe into 4 sections; remove seeds, and peel. Place cantaloupe sections on lettuce-lined plates. Top evenly with grapes; drizzle with mayonnaise mixture. Yield: 4 servings.

Salad Mandarin

PREP: 12 MINUTES

•Store a firm avocado in a paper sack overnight to rush its ripening.

1 medium head Bibb or Boston lettuce, torn
1 (11-ounce) can mandarin oranges, chilled and drained
1 ripe avocado, peeled and thinly sliced

½ cup coarsely chopped pecans, toasted
2 green onions, thinly sliced
Freshly ground pepper to taste
⅓ cup commercial Italian salad dressing

Combine first 6 ingredients in a salad bowl. Add Italian dressing just before serving, and toss gently. Yield: 4 servings.

SALAD MANDARIN

SPINACH SALAD WITH STRAWBERRIES AND PECANS

Spinach Salad with Strawberries and Pecans

PREP: 13 MINUTES

1 (10-ounce) package fresh
   spinach, torn
1 cup strawberries, halved

1 cup pecan halves, toasted
Poppy Seed Dressing

Combine first 3 ingredients; drizzle with Poppy Seed Dressing. Serve immediately. Yield: 6 servings.

Poppy Seed Dressing

$\frac{1}{3}$ cup cider vinegar or white
   vinegar
$\frac{1}{3}$ cup vegetable oil
$\frac{1}{4}$ cup sugar
1 tablespoon Dijon mustard

1 teaspoon salt
$\frac{1}{2}$ teaspoon pepper
1 small onion, coarsely
   chopped
2 teaspoons poppy seeds

Combine first 7 ingredients in container of an electric blender; cover and process until smooth, stopping once to scrape down sides. Stir in poppy seeds. Yield: about $1\frac{1}{3}$ cups.

•Toasted pecans and fresh berries turn this salad into something special. If you're looking for a shortcut, just buy commercial poppy seed dressing.

Spinach-Apple Salad

PREP: 14 MINUTES   **COOK: 4 MINUTES**

- Be sure to trim the long stems from fresh spinach leaves.
- Save time by sprinkling the salad with bacon bits from a jar instead of cooking bacon slices.

4 slices bacon
4 cups tightly packed fresh spinach, trimmed and torn into bite-size pieces (½ pound)
1 large Red Delicious apple, unpeeled, cored, and thinly sliced

⅓ cup mayonnaise
¼ cup frozen orange juice concentrate, thawed and undiluted
Freshly ground pepper

Place bacon on a microwave-safe rack in a baking dish; cover with paper towels. Microwave at HIGH 3 to 4 minutes or until crisp. Crumble bacon, and set aside.

Combine spinach, apple, and bacon in a large bowl. Combine mayonnaise and orange juice concentrate. Add to spinach mixture; toss gently. Sprinkle with pepper. Yield: 4 servings.

Old-Fashioned Sweet Coleslaw

PREP: 7 MINUTES

- Preshredded cabbage is sometimes called *angel hair* on the package. If you have a head of cabbage on hand, chop or shred six cups to use in this recipe.

1 (10-ounce) package finely shredded cabbage (6 cups)
2 large carrots, scraped and shredded
2 tablespoons sugar

½ teaspoon salt
¼ teaspoon pepper
½ cup commercial salad dressing or mayonnaise

Combine cabbage and carrot in a large bowl. Sprinkle with sugar, salt, and pepper; toss gently. Stir in salad dressing. Cover and chill, if desired. Yield: 3 to 4 servings.

BROCCOLI SLAW

Broccoli Slaw

PREP: 5 MINUTES   COOK: 3 MINUTES
CHILL: 4 HOURS

1 cup sugar
½ cup apple cider vinegar or
    white vinegar
¼ cup water

½ teaspoon mustard seeds
½ teaspoon celery seeds
1 (16-ounce) package broccoli
    slaw mix

•There's plenty of sweet syrup to coat this slaw mix. The longer you let it marinate, the better the flavors will be.

Combine first 5 ingredients in a small saucepan; bring to a boil. Boil, stirring constantly, until sugar dissolves. Remove from heat. Place slaw mix in a large bowl. Pour hot syrup mixture over slaw mix, stirring gently. Cover and chill at least 4 hours, stirring occasionally. Serve with a slotted spoon. Yield: 4 to 6 servings.

Avocado-Endive Salad

PREP: 8 MINUTES

•This salad's worthy of good company. It would team nicely with steak and baked potatoes.

3 tablespoons vegetable oil
1 tablespoon lemon juice
1 tablespoon red wine vinegar
1 tablespoon Dijon mustard
½ teaspoon salt

¼ teaspoon pepper
4 heads Belgian endive
1 ripe avocado, peeled and sliced

Combine first 6 ingredients in a jar. Cover tightly; shake vigorously.
  Rinse endive; pat dry, and trim ends. Arrange endive and avocado on individual salad plates; drizzle with dressing. Serve immediately. Yield: 4 servings.

Blue Cheese Tossed Salad

PREP: 12 MINUTES

•Look for a variety of ready-to-use packages of salad greens available in the produce department.

1 (10-ounce) package mixed baby greens or 8 cups loosely packed mixed lettuces

Blue Cheese Vinaigrette

Combine greens and Blue Cheese Vinaigrette in a large bowl. Toss to coat. Serve immediately. Yield: 4 servings.

Blue Cheese Vinaigrette

⅓ cup olive oil
¼ cup crumbled blue cheese
1½ tablespoons white wine vinegar or white vinegar

½ teaspoon dried oregano
⅛ teaspoon salt
⅛ teaspoon freshly ground pepper

Combine all ingredients in a jar; cover tightly, and shake vigorously. Yield: ½ cup.

Garlic-Tarragon Green Salad

PREP: 12 MINUTES

1 large clove garlic, minced
¼ teaspoon salt
⅛ teaspoon freshly ground
    pepper
⅛ teaspoon dry mustard
1 tablespoon tarragon vinegar
¼ cup vegetable oil
3 heads Bibb lettuce, torn

•Since this dressing is light
and versatile, you can use
eight cups of just about
any combination of mixed
salad greens instead of
Bibb lettuce.

Combine first 4 ingredients in a large salad bowl; mash with a fork.
Add vinegar and oil, blending well. Add lettuce; toss gently. Yield: 4
to 6 servings.

Summer Italian Salad

PREP: 10 MINUTES

15 small fresh mushrooms
2 medium-size tomatoes, cut
    into wedges
1 large cucumber, sliced
1 large green pepper, seeded
    and cut into thin strips
1 cup sliced green onions
    (1 bunch)
1 cup commercial Italian salad
    dressing, chilled
Lettuce leaves
Freshly ground pepper
Grated Parmesan cheese

•If you buy a small wedge
of Parmesan, you can
shave "shards" of cheese,
using a vegetable peeler.
This will give you big bites
of flavor in the salad.

Clean mushrooms with a damp paper towel. Snap off stems. Combine mushroom caps, tomatoes, and next 4 ingredients in a large
bowl, tossing gently. Serve salad on lettuce-lined plates. Sprinkle
with freshly ground pepper and cheese. Yield: 6 servings.

Wilted Greens with Bacon Dressing

PREP: 4 MINUTES   COOK: 5 MINUTES

•A wilted salad like this is best if served right after the hot dressing is added.

6 cups mixed salad greens
2 green onions, thinly sliced
4 slices bacon

¼ cup red wine vinegar
¼ cup lemon juice
Coarsely ground pepper

Combine salad greens and onions in a large bowl; set aside.

Cook bacon in a skillet over medium heat until crisp; remove bacon, reserving 2 tablespoons drippings in skillet. Crumble bacon, and set aside. Add vinegar and lemon juice to drippings in skillet; cook 2 minutes. Immediately pour over salad, and toss gently to coat. Sprinkle with bacon and pepper. Serve immediately. Yield: 4 servings.

Asian Pasta Salad

PREP: 10 MINUTES   COOK: 8 MINUTES

•This colorful high-flavored mix also makes a great main-dish salad. Just add chopped cooked chicken.

•One small head of broccoli should yield more than enough flowerets for this salad.

•Dark sesame oil is made from toasted sesame seeds. Use it sparingly—it's intensely flavored. Find it with Oriental ingredients in the grocery store.

8 ounces dried linguine, uncooked
3 cups broccoli flowerets
12 cherry tomatoes, halved
4 green onions, sliced
2 large carrots, scraped and sliced diagonally
¼ cup soy sauce

2 tablespoons sesame seeds, toasted
2 tablespoons brown sugar
2 tablespoons dark sesame oil
1 tablespoon lemon juice
¼ teaspoon hot sauce
1 large clove garlic, minced

Cook pasta according to package directions; drain. Rinse with cold water; drain again. Place pasta in a large bowl. Add broccoli and next 3 ingredients; toss well.

Combine soy sauce and remaining 6 ingredients in a small jar; cover tightly, and shake vigorously. Pour over pasta mixture; toss gently. Yield: 4 servings.

ASIAN PASTA SALAD

Pesto-Tortellini Salad

PREP: 13 MINUTES   COOK: 4 MINUTES

1 (9-ounce) package
      refrigerated spinach- or
      cheese-filled tortellini,
      uncooked
¾ cup broccoli flowerets
⅓ cup sliced pimiento-stuffed
      olives
2 large carrots, scraped and
      sliced

1 small sweet red pepper,
      seeded and cut into thin
      strips
¼ cup commercial pesto sauce
2 tablespoons grated
      Parmesan cheese
2 tablespoons olive oil
1 teaspoon white vinegar
1 clove garlic, crushed

Cook pasta according to package directions; drain. Rinse with cold water; drain again. Combine pasta, broccoli, and next 3 ingredients; set aside.

Combine pesto sauce and remaining 4 ingredients; stir well. Spoon pesto mixture over pasta and vegetables; toss gently. Cover and chill, if desired. Yield: 5 servings.

Presto Pasta Salad

PREP: 6 MINUTES   COOK: 12 MINUTES

•Rotini is a corkscrew-shaped pasta, also called fusilli.

8 ounces dried rotini pasta,
      uncooked
1½ cups broccoli flowerets
1 cup sliced fresh mushrooms
1 large sweet red pepper,
      seeded and cut into 1-inch
      pieces

1 (8-ounce) bottle Caesar
      salad dressing

Cook pasta according to package directions; drain. Rinse with cold water; drain and place in a large bowl. Add broccoli and remaining ingredients to pasta; toss well. Cover and chill, if desired. Yield: 4 servings.

Caesar Tortellini Salad

PREP: 16 MINUTES   COOK: 5 MINUTES

1 (9-ounce) package refrigerated cheese-filled tortellini or ravioli, uncooked
2 cups cherry tomato halves
½ cup chopped purple onion
¼ cup sliced ripe olives
¼ cup refrigerated shredded Parmesan cheese
½ teaspoon pepper
1 medium cucumber, thinly sliced
¾ cup commercial Caesar salad dressing
8 cups shredded romaine lettuce (about 1 head)

• You could also serve this salad as a meatless main dish for two.

Cook pasta according to package directions; drain. Rinse with cold water; drain again. Combine pasta, tomato halves, and next 6 ingredients; toss well. Cover and chill thoroughly. Serve over shredded lettuce. Yield: 4 servings.

Mexican Black Bean Salad

PREP: 6 MINUTES

1 (8-ounce) carton sour cream
¼ cup chopped fresh cilantro
1 tablespoon taco seasoning
1 large head green leaf lettuce, torn (about 10 cups)
2 cups (8 ounces) shredded Cheddar cheese
½ cup chopped purple onion
2 (15-ounce) cans black beans, drained
2 large tomatoes, chopped
Corn chips, crushed

• Taco seasoning is a powdered spice mixture that comes in small packets on the Mexican food aisle.

Combine first 3 ingredients in a large bowl, stirring well. Add lettuce and next 4 ingredients; toss well. Sprinkle with crushed corn chips, and serve immediately. Yield: 6 servings.

Warm Potato and Sausage Salad

PREP: 10 MINUTES   COOK: 20 MINUTES

• Kielbasa is a Polish sausage. Find it packaged in long links.
• Use Andouille or other smoked sausages for a spicier dish, if desired.

3 pounds red potatoes
1 pound kielbasa sausage, sliced
4 green onions, sliced
½ cup dill pickle relish
¼ cup chopped fresh parsley
½ cup olive oil
¼ cup white wine vinegar or white vinegar

1 tablespoon chopped fresh tarragon or 1 teaspoon dried tarragon
1 tablespoon Dijon mustard
1 teaspoon freshly ground pepper
½ teaspoon salt
3 cloves garlic, minced

Cook potatoes in boiling water to cover in a Dutch oven 10 to 15 minutes or until tender; drain and let cool to touch.

Meanwhile, cook sausage in a large nonstick skillet over medium-high heat 4 minutes or until browned. Drain and set aside.

Slice potatoes. Combine potato slices, green onions, pickle relish, and parsley in a large bowl; stir in sausage.

Combine oil and remaining 6 ingredients in a 2-cup glass measuring cup. Microwave at HIGH 1½ minutes or until mixture comes to a boil. Pour hot dressing over potato mixture; toss to coat. Yield: 6 servings.

Taco Salad

PREP: 20 MINUTES   COOK: 5 MINUTES

1 pound ground beef
1 small onion, chopped
1 (16-ounce) can kidney beans, drained
1 (14¾-ounce) can cream-style corn
1 (1¼-ounce) envelope taco seasoning mix
1 (10½-ounce) package corn chips

6 cups torn iceberg lettuce
2 cups (8 ounces) shredded Cheddar cheese
2 tomatoes, chopped
1 (2¼-ounce) can sliced ripe olives, drained
Guacamole

•This recipe includes a wonderful homemade guacamole. If you're short on time, buy commercial guacamole instead.

Brown ground beef and onion in a large skillet over medium heat, stirring until beef crumbles. Drain and return to skillet. Stir in beans, corn, and seasoning mix.

Layer corn chips, ground beef mixture, and torn lettuce evenly on individual salad plates. Top with cheese, tomato, olives, and Guacamole. Yield: 8 servings.

Guacamole

1 (3-ounce) package cream cheese, softened
1 ripe avocado, peeled and mashed
1 (8-ounce) carton sour cream
1½ tablespoons lemon juice

1 tablespoon chopped green chiles (from a can)
¾ teaspoon chili powder
¼ teaspoon salt
¼ teaspoon hot sauce
1 clove garlic, minced

Beat cream cheese at medium speed of an electric mixer until light and fluffy. Add avocado and remaining ingredients; beat mixture just until blended. Yield: 1½ cups.

Basil-Scented Chicken Salad

PREP: 19 MINUTES

• Bruise the basil leaves before you chop them for maximum flavor. Just press the leaves with the back of a spoon.

• It's convenient to use part of a 10-ounce bag of fresh, cleaned spinach for this recipe.

½ cup mayonnaise
2 tablespoons lemon juice
1 tablespoon Dijon mustard
½ teaspoon lemon-pepper seasoning
¼ teaspoon hot sauce
3 cups chopped cooked chicken

½ cup chopped celery
¼ cup shredded fresh basil
2 green onions, chopped (¼ cup)
6 cups torn or shredded fresh spinach
2 tablespoons pine nuts or pecan pieces, toasted

Combine first 5 ingredients, stirring well. Add chicken and next 3 ingredients, and toss gently. Place spinach on individual serving plates; top with chicken mixture. Sprinkle with pine nuts. Yield: 3 servings.

BASIL-SCENTED CHICKEN SALAD

Royal Curried Chicken Salad

PREP: 11 MINUTES   CHILL: 4 HOURS

2 cups chopped cooked
  chicken
½ cup chopped celery
½ cup sliced almonds, toasted
¼ cup sliced water chestnuts
½ pound seedless red grapes
1 (8-ounce) can pineapple
  chunks, drained

¾ cup mayonnaise
1 teaspoon curry powder
2 teaspoons lemon juice
2 teaspoons soy sauce
2 avocados, sliced (optional)

•Try this curried chicken mixture in a sandwich or on lettuce leaves.

Combine first 6 ingredients in a bowl.

  Combine mayonnaise and next 3 ingredients; spoon over chicken mixture, and toss gently. Cover and chill at least 4 hours. Serve salad with avocado, if desired. Yield: 6 servings.

Uptown Turkey Salad

PREP: 20 MINUTES

2½ cups chopped cooked
  turkey
1 cup diced celery
½ cup raisins
2 green onions, thinly sliced
½ cup mayonnaise or salad
  dressing

¼ cup chopped fresh parsley
1 tablespoon dry white wine
½ teaspoon dried tarragon
¼ teaspoon salt
¼ teaspoon pepper
½ cup slivered almonds,
  toasted

•Stir leftover cooked turkey or chicken into this Waldorf-like salad.

Combine first 4 ingredients. Combine mayonnaise and next 5 ingredients, stirring well. Add to chicken mixture, and toss gently. Stir in almonds just before serving. Yield: 4 servings.

Smoked Turkey Salad

PREP: 10 MINUTES

1 pound smoked turkey, chopped
1 sweet red pepper, seeded and cut into strips
4 green onions, diagonally sliced
½ cup chopped walnuts
½ cup vegetable oil
¼ cup raspberry or red wine vinegar

1 teaspoon seasoned salt
1 teaspoon dried Italian seasoning
¼ teaspoon freshly ground pepper
8 cups torn or 1 (10-ounce) package fresh spinach

Combine first 4 ingredients in a large bowl. Combine oil and next 4 ingredients in a jar. Cover tightly, and shake vigorously. Pour over turkey mixture; toss gently. Cover and chill. Place spinach on individual salad plates; top evenly with turkey mixture. Yield: 4 servings.

Bean Salad with Tuna

PREP: 15 MINUTES

¼ cup chopped fresh parsley
2 tablespoons roasted garlic oil or olive oil*
1 tablespoon lemon juice
¾ teaspoon pepper
¼ teaspoon salt
2 large cloves garlic, crushed
1 (15½-ounce) can garbanzo beans (chick-peas), drained
1 (15-ounce) can cannellini or other white beans, drained

1 (12-ounce) can albacore tuna in spring water, drained
4 plum tomatoes, chopped
12 Bibb lettuce leaves (about 1 head)
½ small purple onion, thinly sliced
Freshly ground pepper (optional)

Combine first 6 ingredients in a large bowl; stir well. Add beans, tuna, and chopped tomato; toss gently.

Place lettuce on individual serving plates; top evenly with bean mixture. Top with onion slices, and sprinkle with pepper, if desired. Serve immediately at room temperature, or cover and chill. Yield: 4 servings.

*For roasted garlic oil, we used Wesson.

Aloha Shrimp Salad

PREP: 10 MINUTES   COOK: 5 MINUTES
CHILL: 1 HOUR

4 cups water
1½ pounds peeled medium-
   size fresh shrimp
   (2 pounds unpeeled)
1 cup finely chopped celery
⅓ cup raisins

1 (20-ounce) can unsweetened
   pineapple chunks, drained
½ cup mayonnaise
2 teaspoons curry powder
Leaf lettuce

Bring 4 cups water to a boil; add shrimp, and cook 3 to 5 minutes or until shrimp turn pink. Drain; rinse with cold water.

Combine shrimp, celery, raisins, and pineapple. Combine mayonnaise and curry powder; stir well. Add to shrimp mixture. Cover and chill at least 1 hour before serving. Serve on lettuce-lined plates. Yield: 3 to 4 servings.

BEAN SALAD WITH TUNA

Shrimp Louis

PREP: 12 MINUTES   COOK: 5 MINUTES

5 cups water
1 pound peeled large fresh
     shrimp (1⅓ pounds
     unpeeled)
½ cup mayonnaise
2 tablespoons chili sauce
2 tablespoons whipping cream
     or sour cream
½ teaspoon lemon juice

¼ teaspoon salt
1 green onion, chopped
     (2 tablespoons)
4 cups shredded green leaf
     lettuce
2 hard-cooked eggs, cut into
     wedges
1 large tomato, cut into
     wedges

Bring 5 cups water to a boil; add shrimp, and cook 3 to 5 minutes or until shrimp turn pink. Drain well; rinse with cold water. Chill.

   Combine mayonnaise and next 5 ingredients, stirring well. Place lettuce on a serving platter. Arrange shrimp, eggs, and tomato over lettuce. Spoon dressing over salad. Yield: 4 servings.

Vegetable-Beef Soup

PREP: 4 MINUTES   COOK: 28 MINUTES

•This four-ingredient comfort food sports a thick tomato base. Use spicy vegetable juice if you like hot 'n' spicy soup. (See photo on page 189.)

1 pound ground chuck
1 (46-ounce) can vegetable
     juice
1 (16-ounce) package frozen
     mixed vegetables

1 (1-ounce) envelope onion
     soup mix

Brown ground chuck in a large skillet, stirring until it crumbles. Drain.

   Meanwhile, combine vegetable juice, frozen vegetables, and soup mix in a Dutch oven or 3-quart saucepan; bring to a boil. Add beef. Cover, reduce heat, and simmer 20 minutes. Yield: 9 cups.

   Microwave Directions: To cook meat, crumble ground chuck into a microwave-safe colander; place colander in a 9-inch pieplate. Cover with wax paper, and microwave at HIGH 5 to 6 minutes, stirring once. Drain.

Veggie-Mac Soup

PREP: 4 MINUTES   **COOK: 25 MINUTES**

3 (14½-ounce) cans chicken
   broth, undiluted
1 (16-ounce) package frozen
   mixed vegetables
1 (14½-ounce) can Italian
   stewed tomatoes,
   undrained and chopped
1 (8½-ounce) can whole
   kernel corn, drained

2 tablespoons dried onion
   flakes
¼ teaspoon pepper
2 cloves garlic, minced
½ cup elbow macaroni,
   uncooked

Combine first 7 ingredients in a Dutch oven; cover and bring to a boil. Stir in pasta; reduce heat, and simmer, uncovered, 20 minutes or until pasta is tender. Yield: 8 cups.

White Bean Soup

PREP: 9 MINUTES   **COOK: 22 MINUTES**

1 (16-ounce) can navy beans,
   undrained
1 (15.8-ounce) can Great
   Northern beans, undrained
1 cup water
2 large carrots, scraped and
   diced

¼ cup butter or margarine,
   melted
1 cup chopped cooked ham or
   1 ham hock
⅓ cup chopped green onions
1 bay leaf

Combine beans in a large saucepan; mash slightly with a potato masher or back of a large spoon. Stir in water, and cook over low heat until thoroughly heated.

  Cook carrot in butter in a small skillet over medium-high heat, stirring constantly, until tender. Add carrot, ham, green onions, and bay leaf to bean mixture. Cook over low heat 10 minutes, stirring occasionally. Discard bay leaf before serving. Yield: 5 cups.

EASY TEXAS CHILI

Peppery Potato Soup

PREP: 7 MINUTES COOK: 18 MINUTES

2 cups peeled, cubed potato
½ cup chopped onion
1 (14½-ounce) can ready-to-serve chicken broth
1 cup milk
1 teaspoon butter or margarine
1 teaspoon chopped fresh thyme or ¼ teaspoon dried thyme
¼ teaspoon salt
¼ teaspoon pepper

Combine first 3 ingredients in a saucepan. Bring to a boil; cover, reduce heat, and simmer 10 minutes or until potato is tender. Remove about 1 cup potato from saucepan with a slotted spoon. Mash remaining mixture in saucepan with a potato masher; add reserved potato, milk, and remaining ingredients. Bring to a boil over medium heat, stirring constantly. Yield: 3½ cups.

Easy Texas Chili

PREP: 2 MINUTES COOK: 20 MINUTES

1 pound ground chuck
1 small onion, chopped
1 teaspoon minced garlic
1 (16-ounce) can chili hot beans, undrained
1 (6-ounce) can tomato paste
1½ cups water
1 tablespoon chili powder
1 teaspoon salt

•Crumble tender Sour Cream Cornbread (page 193) into this 20 minute Western chili.

Combine first 3 ingredients in a Dutch oven; cook until beef is browned, stirring until it crumbles. Drain and return to Dutch oven. Add beans and remaining ingredients; cover, reduce heat, and simmer 15 minutes, stirring occasionally. Yield: 6 cups.

Corn Chowder

PREP: 8 MINUTES   COOK: 8 MINUTES

2 (11-ounce) cans Mexican-style corn, drained
1 (10¾-ounce) can cream of potato soup, undiluted
1⅓ cups milk
1 tablespoon butter or margarine
½ teaspoon pepper
4 slices bacon
2 green onions, sliced

Combine first 5 ingredients in a large saucepan. Cook over medium heat until thoroughly heated, stirring occasionally.

  Meanwhile, place bacon on a microwave-safe rack in a baking dish. Cover with paper towels. Microwave at HIGH 4 minutes or until crisp. Drain bacon, and crumble. Sprinkle bacon and green onions over soup. Yield: 4½ cups.

Potato-Cheese Chowder

PREP: 12 MINUTES   COOK: 31 MINUTES

•Cubing the cheese helps speed its melting in this chunky thick soup.

½ cup chopped celery
½ cup chopped onion
½ cup chopped green pepper
¼ cup butter or margarine, melted
3 cups chicken broth
1 medium potato, unpeeled and cubed
1 large carrot, scraped and chopped
½ cup all-purpose flour
2 cups milk, divided
12 ounces sharp American cheese, cubed
2 tablespoons chopped fresh parsley

Cook first 3 ingredients in butter in a Dutch oven over medium-high heat, stirring constantly, until tender. Add broth, potato, and carrot; bring to a boil. Cover, reduce heat, and simmer 20 minutes or until vegetables are tender.

  Combine flour and ¾ cup milk, stirring until smooth. Gradually stir flour mixture into vegetable mixture. Add remaining 1¼ cups milk, cheese, and parsley. Cook over medium-low heat, stirring constantly, 8 minutes or until thickened and bubbly. Serve immediately. Yield: 8 cups.

Ham and Hash Brown Soup

PREP: 10 MINUTES   COOK: 22 MINUTES

2½ cups water
2 cups frozen cubed hash
 brown potatoes
2 cups chopped cooked ham
1½ cups thinly sliced carrots
½ cup chopped green pepper
¼ cup chopped sweet red
 pepper

1 (15-ounce) can cream-style
 corn
1 (11-ounce) can nacho fiesta
 cheese soup, undiluted
½ cup water
Dash of pepper

Combine first 6 ingredients in a Dutch oven; bring to a boil. Cover, reduce heat, and simmer 15 minutes or until vegetables are tender. Add corn and remaining ingredients; cook until thoroughly heated, stirring often. Yield: 8 cups.

HAM AND HASH BROWN SOUP

Turkey-Corn Chowder

PREP: 7 MINUTES   COOK: 32 MINUTES

• For hash browns, we used a bag of Ore-Ida Southern-Style. They're cubed, not shredded.

2 (10-ounce) packages frozen chopped onion or 4 medium onions, chopped
¼ cup butter or margarine, melted
4 celery stalks with leaves
1 (32-ounce) package frozen cubed hash brown potatoes
1 tablespoon salt
¾ teaspoon pepper

1 chicken bouillon cube
2 cups water
3 cups milk
3 cups chopped cooked turkey or chicken
1 cup half-and-half
½ teaspoon dried thyme
2 (15¼-ounce) cans whole kernel corn, drained
1 (14¾-ounce) can cream-style corn

Cook onion in butter in a Dutch oven over medium-high heat, stirring constantly, until tender.

Chop celery, reserving leaves for garnish, if desired. Add chopped celery, frozen hash brown potatoes, and next 4 ingredients to onion mixture; bring to a boil. Cover, reduce heat, and simmer 15 minutes.

Add milk and remaining 5 ingredients; cook until thoroughly heated. Garnish with reserved celery leaves, if desired. Yield: 4 quarts.

Sloppy Joe Loaf

PREP: 5 MINUTES   COOK: 20 MINUTES

¾ pound ground beef
½ cup chopped onion
1 (14½-ounce) can diced tomatoes with garlic and onion, undrained
2 tablespoons brown sugar

2 tablespoons white vinegar
1 (1-pound) loaf Italian bread
1½ cups (6 ounces) shredded nacho-and-taco cheese blend

Brown ground beef and onion in a large skillet over medium heat, stirring until beef crumbles; drain and return to skillet. Add tomatoes, brown sugar, and vinegar; cook, stirring constantly, 3 minutes.

Slice bread in half lengthwise; place on an ungreased baking sheet. Bake at 425° for 5 minutes or until toasted. Spread bread halves with meat mixture, and top with cheese. Bake at 425° for 12 minutes or until cheese melts and loaf is thoroughly heated. Cut each half into 3 pieces. Yield: 6 servings.

Mile-High Sandwich Round

PREP: 15 MINUTES   COOK: 35 MINUTES

1 (1-pound) round loaf bread
½ cup mayonnaise
1½ teaspoons dried Italian seasoning
½ teaspoon pepper
1 large onion, thinly sliced
1 small green pepper, seeded and cut into thin strips

1 stalk celery, sliced
1 tablespoon olive oil
1 (10-ounce) package sliced cooked ham
1½ cups (6 ounces) shredded Cheddar-mozzarella cheese blend

•Choose a soft rather than crusty bread to create this tall sandwich. It'll be easier to eat. Either way, you might find a knife and fork helpful.

Slice off top one-fourth of bread loaf; set top aside. Hollow out bottom, leaving a ½-inch shell.

Combine mayonnaise, Italian seasoning, and pepper. Brush half of mixture inside bread shell. Set aside bread shell and remaining mayonnaise mixture.

Cook onion, green pepper, and celery in oil in a large skillet over medium-high heat, stirring constantly, 5 minutes or until tender.

Arrange half of ham in bread shell, and top with half of vegetable mixture; sprinkle with half of cheese. Top with remaining ham; spread remaining mayonnaise mixture over ham. Top with remaining vegetable mixture and cheese. Replace bread top, and wrap loaf in aluminum foil. Bake at 400° for 30 minutes or until thoroughly heated. Cut into wedges, and serve immediately. Yield: 6 servings.

SLOPPY JOE LOAF

Meatball Hoagies

PREP: 4 MINUTES   COOK: 20 MINUTES

•You can substitute sliced cheese, cut into triangles, for shredded cheese, if desired.

1 (20-ounce) package frozen meatballs*

1 (27.7-ounce) jar spaghetti sauce

1 clove garlic, crushed

1 (15-ounce) package submarine or hoagie rolls, split

1½ cups (6 ounces) shredded mozzarella cheese

Combine first 3 ingredients in a large skillet or saucepan. Cover and cook 20 minutes over medium heat, stirring occasionally. Spoon evenly onto bottoms of rolls; top with cheese and roll tops. Serve immediately. Yield: 6 servings.

*For frozen meatballs, we used Armour.

MEATBALL HOAGIE

Easy Pocket Pizzas

PREP: 14 MINUTES   **COOK: 10 MINUTES**

1 cup commercial pizza sauce
4 (6- or 7-inch) pita bread
   rounds, cut in half
1 (3½-ounce) package sliced
   pepperoni

1½ cups (6 ounces) shredded
   mozzarella cheese
2 tablespoons grated
   Parmesan cheese

•Kids will devour these
thin pepperoni sandwiches.

Spread 2 tablespoons pizza sauce inside each pita half. Arrange 6 slices pepperoni inside each half. Sprinkle cheeses evenly in pockets. Place pockets on a baking sheet. Bake at 400° for 8 to 10 minutes. Serve immediately. Yield: 4 servings.

Chicken-Cheese French Bread Pizzas

PREP: 15 MINUTES   **COOK: 10 MINUTES**

½ cup butter or margarine,
   softened
½ cup (2 ounces) shredded
   Cheddar cheese
⅓ cup freshly grated
   Parmesan cheese
¼ teaspoon dried Italian
   seasoning
1 clove garlic, crushed
1 (16-ounce) loaf sliced
   French bread

1 (10-ounce) can white
   chicken, drained and
   flaked
1 cup (4 ounces) shredded
   mozzarella cheese
½ cup chopped sweet red
   pepper
2 green onions, chopped
   (¼ cup)

•There should be 13 or 14
slices of French bread in
the loaf, so each serving is
at least two slices.

•You can substitute 1½
cups chopped cooked
chicken breast for the
canned chicken.

Combine first 5 ingredients; spread evenly over bread slices. Top with chicken; sprinkle with mozzarella cheese, red pepper, and green onions. Bake at 350° for 10 minutes or until cheese melts. Yield: 6 servings.

DRESSED-UP
ROAST BEEF SANDWICH

Dressed-Up Roast Beef Sandwiches

PREP: 11 MINUTES

•Hoagie rolls are available with or without sesame seeds. You choose.

4 (2-ounce) hoagie rolls, split
1 (3-ounce) package cream cheese, softened
2 tablespoons mayonnaise
2 tablespoons chutney
2 teaspoons prepared horseradish
4 lettuce leaves

12 ounces thinly sliced roast beef
2 medium tomatoes, sliced
4 ounces mozzarella cheese, thinly sliced
Freshly ground pepper
2 slices purple onion, separated into rings

Toast rolls, if desired. Combine cream cheese and next 3 ingredients; spread on bottoms of rolls. Place lettuce leaves on cream cheese mixture; top evenly with roast beef, tomato slices, and cheese. Sprinkle with pepper. Add onion; cover with roll tops. Serve immediately; or wrap each sandwich tightly in heavy-duty plastic wrap, and chill up to 4 hours. Yield: 4 servings.

Reuben Salad Sandwiches

1 (12-ounce) can corned beef
1 (14.5-ounce) can or 1 (16-
  ounce) jar sauerkraut,
  well drained
½ cup commercial Thousand
  Island salad dressing
½ teaspoon pepper
1 tablespoon bacon bits
8 slices rye bread, toasted
4 slices Swiss cheese

Crumble corned beef with a fork. Add sauerkraut and next 3 ingredients, stirring well. Spread mixture on 4 toast slices. Top each sandwich with cheese. Bake at 350° for 10 minutes or until cheese melts. Top with remaining toast. Yield: 4 servings.

Mexican Roast Beef Roll-Ups

8 (9-inch) flour tortillas
½ cup sour cream
¼ cup mayonnaise or salad
  dressing
3 tablespoons hot salsa
1 pound thinly sliced roast
  beef
8 large lettuce leaves
Additional salsa

•Refrigerated flour tortillas vary in size. Look for large ones for these beefy roll-ups.

Heat tortillas according to package directions. Combine sour cream, mayonnaise, and 3 tablespoons salsa, stirring well; spread over tortillas. Arrange roast beef and lettuce leaves neatly on tortillas. Roll up tortillas, jellyroll fashion; secure with wooden picks. Slice each tortilla roll in half. Serve with additional salsa. Yield: 4 servings.

Chicken-Pecan Pitas

PREP: 7 MINUTES

•Use deli-roasted or smoked chicken in this recipe for extra flavor.

2 cups chopped cooked chicken
½ cup seedless red grapes
½ cup chopped pecans, toasted
¼ cup mayonnaise or salad dressing

2 tablespoons sour cream
1 tablespoon fresh lime juice
2 large pita bread rounds, cut in half
4 red leaf lettuce leaves

Combine first 3 ingredients. Combine mayonnaise, sour cream, and lime juice; stir into chicken mixture. Line pita bread halves with lettuce leaves, and fill with chicken mixture. Yield: 4 servings.

Open-Faced Olive-Chicken Salad Sandwiches

PREP: 12 MINUTES   **COOK: 3 MINUTES**

•Tangy green olives are a pleasant surprise in this chicken salad.

2 (5-ounce) cans chunk white chicken in water, drained
½ cup chopped celery
⅓ cup chopped pimiento-stuffed olives
⅓ cup mayonnaise
3 tablespoons minced fresh parsley

½ teaspoon pepper
2 hard-cooked eggs, chopped
4 English muffins, split and toasted
1 cup (4 ounces) shredded Swiss cheese

Combine first 7 ingredients, stirring well. Spread evenly over muffin halves, and place on a baking sheet. Sprinkle with cheese. Broil 5½ inches from heat (with electric oven door partially opened) 3 minutes or until cheese melts. Yield: 8 servings.

Chicken-Avocado Dagwoods

PREP: 25 MINUTES   **COOK: 8 MINUTES**

8 slices bacon

Mayonnaise

8 slices sourdough bread,
   toasted

2 ripe avocados, peeled and
   mashed

8 slices purple onion

4 (1-ounce) slices Monterey
   Jack or provolone cheese

8 lettuce leaves

8 slices tomato

8 (¼-inch-thick) slices roasted
   chicken breast

⅛ teaspoon salt

⅛ teaspoon pepper

Garnish: sweet pickles

• Mash avocados the clean and easy way: Place peeled halves in a heavy-duty, zip-top plastic bag; seal bag, and squeeze.

Place bacon on a microwave-safe rack in a baking dish; cover with paper towels. Microwave at HIGH 8 minutes or until bacon is crisp. Drain bacon, and set aside.

Spread mayonnaise on toast; layer mashed avocado, bacon, onion, and next 4 ingredients on 4 slices toast. Sprinkle with salt and pepper. Top with remaining toast. Garnish, if desired. Serve immediately. Yield: 4 servings.

CHICKEN-AVOCADO DAGWOOD

Chicken-Biscuit Melts

PREP: 12 MINUTES   COOK: 14 MINUTES

• Pair these big Mexican biscuits with a cup of black bean soup or chili for a filling meal.

1 (17.3-ounce) can refrigerated large biscuits*
3 (5-ounce) cans chunk white chicken in water, drained, or 1½ cups chopped cooked chicken
⅔ cup picante sauce
½ teaspoon ground cumin

1 (4.5-ounce) can diced green chiles, drained
1 bunch green onions, sliced
2 cups (8 ounces) shredded colby-Monterey Jack cheese blend
Additional picante sauce
Sour cream

Bake biscuits according to package directions; split and place on a baking sheet. Set aside.

Combine chicken and next 4 ingredients in a saucepan; cook mixture over medium heat 5 minutes or until thoroughly heated, stirring often. Spoon mixture over biscuits, and sprinkle with cheese.

Broil 5½ inches from heat (with electric oven door partially opened) 2 to 3 minutes or until cheese melts. Serve with additional picante sauce and sour cream. Yield: 8 servings.

*For biscuits, we used Grands.

Cordon Bleu Croissants

PREP: 11 MINUTES   COOK: 12 MINUTES

• For this recipe look for large croissants, usually four per package, instead of petite croissants with six per package.

2 (6-ounce) packages frozen large croissants
2½ tablespoons prepared horseradish
8 thin slices cooked ham

8 thin slices cooked chicken breast
8 slices Swiss cheese

Split each croissant in half; spread bottoms of croissants evenly with horseradish. Layer 1 slice each of ham, chicken, and Swiss cheese over horseradish. Cover with croissant tops. Place croissant sandwiches on a large baking sheet. Bake at 325° for 12 minutes or until thoroughly heated. Yield: 8 servings.

Hot Chicken Salad Sandwiches

PREP: 13 MINUTES   COOK: 7 MINUTES

2 (5-ounce) cans chunk white chicken, drained and flaked
1 (8-ounce) can pineapple tidbits, drained
1 cup (4 ounces) shredded sharp Cheddar cheese
¼ cup finely chopped green pepper
2 tablespoons finely chopped celery
1 tablespoon finely chopped onion
⅓ cup mayonnaise
½ teaspoon salt
3 kaiser rolls, split

•You can substitute 1½ cups chopped cooked chicken for canned chicken, if desired.

Combine first 8 ingredients, stirring well. Place rolls on a baking sheet. Broil 5½ inches from heat (with electric oven door partially opened) 2 minutes or until lightly browned. Spread filling evenly over rolls. Bake at 350° for 5 minutes or until thoroughly heated. Yield: 6 servings.

Spicy Chicken Pitas

PREP: 11 MINUTES   MARINATE: 30 MINUTES
GRILL: 12 MINUTES

6 skinned and boned chicken breast halves
1 tablespoon Creole seasoning
1 tablespoon vegetable oil
½ cup mayonnaise
4 (6-inch) whole wheat pita bread rounds, cut in half
8 lettuce leaves
1 small onion, thinly sliced and separated into rings
1 cup alfalfa sprouts
¾ cup chopped cucumber
¾ cup chopped tomato

•You can make your own Creole seasoning with just a few ingredients you probably have on hand. Combine 1 teaspoon paprika, ¾ teaspoon garlic powder, ½ teaspoon dried thyme, ½ teaspoon salt, and ½ teaspoon ground red pepper.

Coat chicken with Creole seasoning. Cover and marinate in refrigerator at least 30 minutes. Drizzle oil over chicken.

Grill chicken, covered with grill lid, over medium-hot coals (350° to 400°) 5 to 6 minutes on each side or until done. Let cool slightly. Cut chicken into strips.

Spread 1 tablespoon mayonnaise inside each pita half. Line with lettuce. Arrange chicken evenly in pita halves. Add onion and remaining ingredients. Yield: 8 servings.

CHICKEN CROISSANT MELT

Chicken Croissant Melts

PREP: 11 MINUTES   COOK: 5 MINUTES

•Croissants give this sprouts and avocado sandwich upscale appeal.

4 slices bacon
1 (3-ounce) package cream cheese, softened
1 tablespoon grated Parmesan cheese
1 tablespoon minced onion
1 tablespoon sour cream
4 large croissants, split

6 ounces thinly sliced cooked chicken or turkey
2 tomatoes, sliced
1 ripe avocado, sliced
8 slices process American cheese
Alfalfa sprouts

Place bacon on a microwave-safe rack in a baking dish; cover with paper towels. Microwave at HIGH 3 to 4 minutes or until bacon is crisp. Drain and crumble bacon.

Combine bacon, cream cheese, and next 3 ingredients, stirring until blended. Spread on cut sides of croissants.

Layer chicken and next 3 ingredients on bottoms of croissants, and place on a baking sheet. Broil 5½ inches from heat (with electric oven door partially opened) 1 minute or until cheese melts. Top with alfalfa sprouts and croissant tops. Serve immediately. Yield: 4 servings.

Turkey Sub with Garlic Mayonnaise

PREP: 10 MINUTES

¼ cup mayonnaise
1 tablespoon Dijon mustard
2 cloves garlic, crushed
1 (16-ounce) loaf unsliced French bread, cut in half lengthwise
Lettuce leaves

12 ounces sliced cooked turkey
2 medium tomatoes, sliced
1 cup loosely packed alfalfa sprouts
1 small purple onion, sliced

Combine first 3 ingredients, stirring well; spread on cut sides of bread. Layer lettuce and remaining ingredients on bottom bread half; cover with bread top. Cut loaf into slices. Yield: 6 servings.

Monte Cristo Sandwiches

PREP: 10 MINUTES   COOK: 24 MINUTES

1½ tablespoons mayonnaise
¾ teaspoon prepared mustard
6 slices sandwich bread, trimmed
3 slices cooked turkey
3 slices cooked ham
3 slices Swiss cheese
1 large egg, lightly beaten

½ cup milk
¾ cup pancake mix
3 tablespoons butter or margarine
Sifted powdered sugar (optional)
Strawberry preserves (optional)

Combine mayonnaise and mustard; spread on 1 side of each bread slice. Place 1 slice turkey, ham, and cheese on 3 bread slices. Top with remaining bread. Cut each sandwich in half diagonally, and secure with wooden picks.

Combine egg and milk in a shallow dish. Add pancake mix, stirring until blended. Dip each sandwich into batter.

Melt butter in a large heavy skillet, griddle, or electric skillet; add sandwiches, and cook 4 minutes on each side or until lightly browned. Serve with powdered sugar and strawberry preserves, if desired. Yield: 3 sandwiches.

Turkey-Asparagus Sandwiches

PREP: 7 MINUTES   COOK: 12 MINUTES

• These open-facers are smothered in melted Cheddar and hollandaise—knife-and-fork sandwiches, for sure.

¾ pound fresh asparagus or 1 (10-ounce) package frozen asparagus spears
1 (0.9-ounce) package hollandaise sauce mix

3 English muffins, split and toasted
¾ pound thinly sliced turkey
6 slices Cheddar cheese
Paprika (optional)

Snap off tough ends of asparagus. Cut each asparagus spear in half. Arrange asparagus in a steamer basket over boiling water; cover and steam 4 minutes or until crisp-tender.

Prepare hollandaise sauce mix according to package directions; set aside, and keep warm.

Place muffin halves, cut side up, on a baking sheet. Place turkey on muffin halves; top with asparagus and cheese. Broil 5½ inches from heat (with electric oven door partially opened) 2 to 3 minutes or until cheese melts. Place sandwiches on plates. Pour hollandaise sauce over sandwiches. Sprinkle with paprika, if desired. Yield: 6 servings.

Tuna Burgers

PREP: 13 MINUTES   COOK: 40 MINUTES

• Two kinds of bread-crumbs contribute to this burger. Fresh crumbs (from fresh bread slices) add soft texture to the inside of the burger. Dry crumbs (from a can) become a crispy coating during baking.

1 (9-ounce) can solid white tuna in spring water, undrained and flaked
½ cup soft fresh breadcrumbs
¼ cup finely chopped green pepper
2 tablespoons finely chopped celery
2 tablespoons finely chopped onion

2 tablespoons milk
¼ teaspoon salt
⅛ teaspoon pepper
1 large egg, lightly beaten
½ cup fine, dry breadcrumbs
4 hamburger buns, toasted
Tomato slices
Lettuce leaves
Onion slices
Tartar sauce

Combine first 9 ingredients in a large bowl; shape into 4 patties. Coat patties with dry breadcrumbs, and place on a lightly greased 15- x 10- x 1-inch jellyroll pan. Bake at 350° for 40 minutes or until lightly browned. Serve on buns with tomato and remaining ingredients. Yield: 4 servings.

Curried Tuna Melts

PREP: 10 MINUTES   COOK: 4 MINUTES

1 (6-ounce) can solid white
   tuna in spring water,
   drained and flaked
1 cup (4 ounces) shredded
   Monterey Jack cheese
⅓ cup mayonnaise
½ teaspoon curry powder
¼ teaspoon salt

¼ teaspoon pepper
3 hard-cooked eggs, chopped
2 green onions, chopped (¼
   cup)
8 slices rye bread
1 tablespoon butter or
   margarine

Combine first 8 ingredients in a bowl, stirring well. Spread mixture on 4 bread slices. Top with remaining bread slices.

  Melt butter in a nonstick skillet or griddle over medium heat. Add sandwiches. Cook 2 minutes on each side or until sandwiches are golden. Serve immediately. Yield: 4 servings.

Tuna Roll Sandwiches

PREP: 20 MINUTES   CHILL: 1 HOUR

1 (3-ounce) package cream
   cheese, softened
2 tablespoons mayonnaise
1 tablespoon lemon juice
½ teaspoon pepper
¼ teaspoon salt

1 (10-ounce) can solid white
   tuna in spring water,
   drained and flaked
½ cup chopped purple onion
6 lettuce leaves
6 (8-inch) flour tortillas

Combine first 5 ingredients, stirring until smooth. Add tuna and onion, stirring well.

  Place lettuce on tortillas; spoon tuna mixture onto lettuce. Roll up, and tie with string. Wrap in plastic wrap, and chill 1 hour before serving. Yield: 6 servings.

Grilled Chili con Queso Sandwiches

PREP: 4 MINUTES   COOK: 6 MINUTES

• This is a tall, deluxe grilled cheese sandwich.

½ (8-ounce) block Monterey Jack cheese with peppers
4 (¾-inch-thick) diagonal slices French bread

6 plum tomato slices
1 tablespoon butter or margarine, softened

Cut cheese into 8 lengthwise slices. Arrange 2 slices of cheese each on 2 bread slices; top each with 3 tomato slices and 2 more cheese slices. Top with remaining bread slices.

Spread half of butter on tops of sandwiches. Invert sandwiches onto a hot nonstick skillet or griddle, and cook over medium heat until browned. Spread remaining butter on ungrilled sides of sandwiches; turn and cook until browned. Serve immediately. Yield: 2 servings.

Welsh Rarebit with Tomatoes and Bacon

PREP: 7 MINUTES   COOK: 12 MINUTES

1½ (8-ounce) loaves process cheese spread
1 tablespoon butter or margarine
½ cup beer
1 teaspoon Worcestershire sauce

½ teaspoon dry mustard
⅛ teaspoon ground red pepper
6 slices bacon
3 medium tomatoes, sliced
6 slices bread, toasted

Melt process cheese spread and butter in a large heavy saucepan over medium-low heat, stirring until blended. Gradually add beer, stirring constantly. Stir in Worcestershire sauce, mustard, and red pepper. Cook until thoroughly heated.

Meanwhile, place bacon on a microwave-safe rack in a baking dish. Cover with paper towels. Microwave at HIGH 5 to 6 minutes. Drain and crumble bacon.

Arrange tomato slices over toast; spoon cheese mixture evenly over tomato slices, and sprinkle with bacon. Yield: 6 servings.

PAGE 156

PAGE 181

Simple Side Dishes

PAGE 161

PAGE 177

THESE FAST AND FRESH SIDE DISHES PROVE THAT VEGGIES, PASTA, AND RICE DON'T HAVE TO BE OVERSHADOWED BY THE MEAT. YOU'LL TURN TO THESE QUICK-FIX SIDES NIGHT AFTER NIGHT TO ROUND OUT YOUR MEAL.

PAGE 174

PAGE 173

ASPARAGUS WITH
JALAPEÑO HOLLANDAISE

Asparagus with Jalapeño Hollandaise

PREP: 4 MINUTES   COOK: 15 MINUTES

•This classic egg- and butter-enriched cream sauce is made easier using a packaged mix, and the jalapeño spices it up.

1½ pounds fresh asparagus spears
¼ cup water
1 (0.9-ounce) package hollandaise sauce mix
2 tablespoons grated Parmesan cheese

1 jalapeño pepper, seeded and chopped
1 (2-ounce) jar diced or sliced pimiento, drained

Snap off tough ends of asparagus. Cook asparagus in water in a large skillet over medium heat 4 to 6 minutes; drain. Arrange asparagus on a serving platter; set aside, and keep warm.

Prepare hollandaise sauce mix according to package directions. Stir in cheese, jalapeño pepper, and pimiento. Serve over warm asparagus. Yield: 6 servings.

Microwave Directions: Arrange asparagus in an 11- x 7- x 1½-inch baking dish with stem ends toward outside of dish; add water. Cover with heavy-duty plastic wrap, and microwave at HIGH 8 to 10 minutes or until crisp-tender. Let stand, covered, 1 minute; drain and serve as directed.

Asparagus with Citrus Sauce

PREP: 5 MINUTES   COOK: 10 MINUTES

¼ cup butter or margarine
½ teaspoon grated lemon rind
  or orange rind
2 tablespoons lemon juice or
  orange juice

1½ pounds fresh asparagus
  spears
¼ cup water
¼ cup sliced almonds, toasted

Combine first 3 ingredients in a saucepan. Cook over low heat until butter melts; keep warm.

Snap off tough ends of asparagus. Cook asparagus in water in a large skillet over medium heat 4 to 6 minutes; drain. Arrange asparagus on a serving platter. Pour warm sauce over asparagus, and top with almonds. Yield: 6 servings.

Microwave Directions: Arrange asparagus in an 11- x 7- x 1½-inch baking dish with stem ends toward outside of dish; add ¼ cup water. Cover with heavy-duty plastic wrap, and microwave at HIGH 8 to 10 minutes or until crisp-tender. Let stand, covered, 1 minute; drain and serve as directed.

Asparagus Vinaigrette

PREP: 5 MINUTES   **COOK: 6 MINUTES**

MARINATE: UP TO 8 HOURS

•The bright green aspara-
gus may darken the longer
it marinates in this tangy
vinaigrette, but the flavor
will be enhanced.

1 pound fresh asparagus
⅓ cup tarragon wine vinegar
   or white wine vinegar
1 tablespoon lemon juice
1 tablespoon chopped green
   onion

½ teaspoon dried tarragon
½ teaspoon Dijon mustard
⅛ teaspoon salt
1 clove garlic, crushed

Snap off tough ends of asparagus. Arrange asparagus in a steamer basket over boiling water. Cover and steam 6 minutes or until crisp-tender. Transfer to a serving bowl, and set aside.

   Combine vinegar and remaining 6 ingredients; pour over asparagus. Cover and marinate in refrigerator 30 minutes or up to 8 hours. Yield: 4 servings.

Asparagus Stir-Fry

PREP: 4 MINUTES   **COOK: 12 MINUTES**

•To toast cashews, bake
them at 350° for 3 to 5
minutes.

1½ pounds fresh asparagus
   spears
1 tablespoon vegetable oil
¾ cup water, divided
¾ teaspoon chicken bouillon
   granules

1 tablespoon cornstarch
1 teaspoon sugar
2 tablespoons soy sauce
1 (2-ounce) package cashews,
   coarsely chopped and
   toasted (about ½ cup)

Snap off tough ends of asparagus. Cut spears into 1-inch pieces.

   Cook asparagus in oil in a large skillet over medium-high heat, stirring constantly, 3 minutes. Add ¼ cup water; cover and cook 4 minutes or until crisp-tender.

   Combine remaining ½ cup water, bouillon granules, and next 3 ingredients, stirring until smooth. Add to asparagus, stirring constantly. Bring to a boil; cook, stirring constantly, 1 minute. Sprinkle with cashews, and serve immediately. Yield: 6 servings.

Buttered Green Beans

PREP: 5 MINUTES   COOK: 12 MINUTES

1½ pounds fresh green beans
¾ cup water

¼ cup butter or margarine
Salt and pepper to taste

Trim ends from green beans, and remove strings.

  Bring water to a boil in a large saucepan; add beans. Cover, reduce heat, and simmer 10 to 12 minutes or until crisp-tender, stirring occasionally. Drain beans; add butter, salt, and pepper. Toss until butter melts. Yield: 6 servings.

Garlic Green Beans

PREP: 6 MINUTES   COOK: 15 MINUTES

1 pound fresh green beans
½ cup water
3 tablespoons butter or
   margarine

3 or 4 cloves garlic, minced
⅛ teaspoon salt
⅛ teaspoon pepper
⅓ cup chopped fresh parsley

Trim ends from green beans, and remove strings.

  Bring ½ cup water to a boil in a large saucepan. Add beans; cover, reduce heat, and simmer 8 to 10 minutes, stirring occasionally. Drain beans; rinse with cold water, and set aside.

  Melt butter in a large skillet over medium-high heat; add garlic, and cook, stirring constantly, 1 minute. Add beans, salt, and pepper. Cook over medium heat 3 minutes or until thoroughly heated, stirring occasionally. Stir in parsley. Yield: 4 servings.

Green Bean Vinaigrette

PREP: 5 MINUTES   COOK: 8 MINUTES
CHILL: 1 HOUR

1 (16-ounce) package frozen
    French-cut green beans
½ cup finely chopped onion
¼ cup sliced ripe olives
¼ cup olive oil
2 tablespoons cider vinegar or
    white vinegar
¾ teaspoon dried tarragon

¼ teaspoon dried basil
¼ teaspoon salt
¼ teaspoon pepper
1 clove garlic, minced
¼ cup freshly grated
    Parmesan cheese
Sliced tomatoes

Cook green beans according to package directions; drain. Plunge beans into ice water to stop the cooking process. Drain and set aside.

Combine onion and next 8 ingredients in a bowl; add beans, tossing to coat. Cover and chill 1 hour.

Sprinkle beans with cheese. Serve with tomatoes. Yield: 6 servings.

GREEN BEAN
VINAIGRETTE

Tangy Green Beans

PREP: 2 MINUTES   COOK: 9 MINUTES

4 slices bacon, cut into ½-inch
    pieces
½ cup chopped onion
2 (14½-ounce) cans whole
    green beans, undrained

3 tablespoons white vinegar
½ teaspoon beef bouillon
    granules
¼ teaspoon pepper

Cook bacon in a large skillet until lightly browned. Add onion, and cook, stirring constantly, until onion is tender and bacon is crisp.

  Drain green beans, reserving ¾ cup liquid. Add beans and reserved liquid to bacon mixture in skillet; stir in vinegar, bouillon granules, and pepper. Cook over medium heat until thoroughly heated, stirring gently. Yield: 6 servings.

Limas in Sour Cream

PREP: 3 MINUTES   COOK: 21 MINUTES

2 tablespoons butter or
    margarine
2 tablespoons chopped onion
2 (10-ounce) packages frozen
    baby lima beans
1 (8-ounce) carton sour cream

½ teaspoon salt
¼ teaspoon pepper
1 (2-ounce) jar diced
    pimiento, drained
    (optional)

•These limas are smothered in sour cream and simple seasonings. They're easy to fix, and great taste follows.

Melt butter in a saucepan; add onion, and cook, stirring constantly, until tender. Set aside.

  Cook beans according to package directions; drain. Add to onion mixture in saucepan. Stir in sour cream, salt, and pepper. Add pimiento, if desired. Cook over low heat just until thoroughly heated. Serve immediately. Yield: 6 servings.

English Walnut Broccoli

PREP: 9 MINUTES   **COOK: 27 MINUTES**

1 (10-ounce) package frozen chopped broccoli, thawed and drained
3½ tablespoons butter or margarine, divided
2 tablespoons all-purpose flour

1 teaspoon chicken bouillon granules
1 cup milk
2½ tablespoons water
¾ cup herb-seasoned stuffing mix
¼ cup chopped walnuts

Arrange broccoli in a lightly greased 1-quart baking dish; set aside.

Melt 2 tablespoons butter in a saucepan over low heat; add flour and bouillon granules, stirring until smooth. Cook, stirring constantly, 1 minute. Gradually add milk; cook over medium heat, stirring constantly, until thickened and bubbly. Pour over broccoli.

Combine water and remaining 1½ tablespoons butter in a saucepan; cook over low heat until butter melts. Stir in stuffing mix and walnuts. Spoon over broccoli mixture. Bake, uncovered, at 350° for 20 minutes. Yield: 3 to 4 servings.

Cheddar-Broccoli Casserole

PREP: 9 MINUTES   **COOK: 30 MINUTES**

•You can make this up to a day ahead; then sprinkle the casserole with stuffing mix and paprika right before baking.

2 (10-ounce) packages frozen chopped broccoli, thawed and drained
1 (10¾-ounce) can cream of mushroom soup, undiluted
1 cup (4 ounces) shredded Cheddar cheese

1 cup mayonnaise
½ teaspoon garlic salt
2 large eggs, lightly beaten
½ cup herb-seasoned stuffing mix
Paprika

Combine first 6 ingredients in a lightly greased 11- x 7- x 1½-inch baking dish; cover and chill, if desired. Sprinkle with seasoned stuffing mix and paprika. Bake, uncovered, at 350° for 30 minutes. Yield: 6 servings.

Dilled Brussels Sprouts

PREP: 2 MINUTES COOK: 10 MINUTES

1 (16-ounce) package frozen
    brussels sprouts
¾ cup commercial zesty
    Italian dressing

1 tablespoon chopped fresh
    dill or 1 teaspoon dried
    dillweed
2 green onions, sliced

Cook brussels sprouts according to package directions; drain well. Combine brussels sprouts, dressing, dill, and green onions, tossing gently. Serve immediately, or cover and chill 30 minutes. Yield: 4 servings.

Lemon-Splashed Vegetables

PREP: 5 MINUTES COOK: 21 MINUTES

2 (10-ounce) packages
    boil-in-bag brussels
    sprouts in butter sauce
1 small head cauliflower,
    broken into flowerets

3 large carrots, scraped and
    diagonally sliced
1 tablespoon lemon juice
½ teaspoon salt
¼ teaspoon pepper

•The sauce is already in these bags of brussels sprouts. Cook all the vegetables in one pan; then open the bag of brussels sprouts, and distribute the butter sauce.

Cook brussels sprouts in bags in a large saucepan in boiling water to cover 8 minutes. Add cauliflower; cook 5 more minutes. Add carrot slices, and cook 5 more minutes. Drain vegetables.

  Combine cauliflower, carrot slices, lemon juice, salt, and pepper in a large serving bowl. Open brussels sprouts bags carefully, and add sprouts with butter sauce to bowl. Toss to coat. Yield: 8 servings.

**ALMOND-VEGETABLE
STIR-FRY**

Almond-Vegetable Stir-Fry

PREP: 6 MINUTES   COOK: 15 MINUTES

1 tablespoon peanut oil
2 large carrots, scraped and
      thinly sliced
½ pound fresh green beans,
      trimmed and cut into
      1-inch pieces
1 cup cauliflower flowerets
4 green onions, sliced
1 sweet red pepper, seeded
      and cut into thin strips

1 cup water
2 teaspoons cornstarch
1 teaspoon chicken bouillon
      granules
¼ teaspoon garlic powder
1 (2.25-ounce) package sliced
      almonds, toasted

Heat oil in a wok or large nonstick skillet over medium-high heat 1
minute. Add carrot slices and beans; stir-fry 5 minutes. Add cauliflower, green onions, and red pepper to skillet; stir-fry 4 minutes.

  Combine water and next 3 ingredients, stirring until smooth. Add to
vegetables; cook, stirring constantly, 3 to 4 minutes or until thickened.
Add almonds; stir-fry 1 minute. Yield: 4 servings.

Honey-Kissed Carrots

PREP: 10 MINUTES   COOK: 12 MINUTES

1 pound carrots, scraped and
  cut into ½-inch slices
⅓ cup golden raisins

⅓ cup honey
2 tablespoons butter or
  margarine

Cook carrot slices in a small amount of boiling water 10 minutes or
until tender; drain and return carrot slices to saucepan. Add raisins,
honey, and butter; cook over low heat until thoroughly heated, stirring occasionally. Yield: 4 servings.

Lemon-Glazed Carrots

PREP: 12 MINUTES   COOK: 14 MINUTES

2 pounds carrots, scraped and
  diagonally sliced
¼ cup butter or margarine
¼ cup firmly packed brown
  sugar

¼ cup lemon juice
½ teaspoon salt

Cook carrot slices in a small amount of boiling water 12 minutes or
until crisp-tender; drain. Melt butter in a small saucepan; add brown
sugar, lemon juice, and salt. Bring to a boil, stirring constantly. Pour over
carrot slices, and toss gently. Serve with a slotted spoon. Yield: 8 servings.

Orange-Glazed Carrots

PREP: 3 MINUTES   COOK: 13 MINUTES

2 (9-ounce) packages frozen
  whole baby carrots
2 tablespoons brown sugar
2 teaspoons cornstarch

¼ teaspoon ground ginger
¼ teaspoon salt
¾ cup orange juice

Cook carrots according to package directions, omitting salt; drain
carrots, and set aside.

Combine brown sugar and remaining 4 ingredients in a saucepan,
stirring until smooth. Bring to a boil over medium heat; cook, stirring
constantly, 1 minute. Add carrots; cook 2 more minutes. Yield: 4 servings.

Freezer-Fresh Creamed Corn

PREP: 3 MINUTES   COOK: 27 MINUTES

•You won't believe this delectably sweet creamed corn starts with frozen kernels.

3 (16-ounce) packages frozen shoepeg corn, partially thawed
½ cup butter or margarine

2 cups milk
1½ to 2 teaspoons salt
½ teaspoon pepper

Position knife blade in food processor bowl; add 1 package of corn. Process until smooth, stopping once to scrape down sides.

Melt butter in a large skillet over medium heat. Stir in pureed corn, remaining 2 packages of corn, milk, salt, and pepper. Bring mixture to a boil, stirring constantly. Reduce heat, and simmer 20 to 25 minutes or until liquid is absorbed, stirring often. Yield: 10 to 12 servings.

Corn and Zucchini

PREP: 3 MINUTES   COOK: 5 MINUTES

1 (16-ounce) package frozen whole kernel corn or 4 cups fresh corn kernels
1 large zucchini, cut into ¼-inch slices
¼ cup butter or margarine, melted

4 green onions, sliced
1 medium tomato, chopped
1 tablespoon chopped fresh parsley
½ teaspoon salt
⅛ teaspoon pepper

Cook corn and zucchini in butter in a large skillet over medium-high heat, stirring constantly, 4 minutes. Add green onions and remaining ingredients. Cook, stirring constantly, 1 minute. Yield: 4 to 6 servings.

Curried Corn and Sweet Red Pepper

PREP: 2 MINUTES   COOK: 8 MINUTES

3 tablespoons butter or
   margarine
¼ cup chopped sweet red
   pepper
1 (15.25-ounce) can whole
   kernel corn, drained

1 teaspoon curry powder
⅛ teaspoon salt
⅛ teaspoon pepper
¼ cup whipping cream

• This corn dish has flavor reminiscent of Native American food. Serve it with sliced pork tenderloin.

Melt butter in a skillet over medium heat; add red pepper, and cook, stirring constantly, until tender. Stir in corn and next 3 ingredients; cook 3 minutes, stirring often. Stir in whipping cream; cook, stirring constantly, until thickened. Yield: 2 to 3 servings.

CURRIED CORN AND
SWEET RED PEPPER

Chilicorn

PREP: 1 MINUTE   COOK: 4 MINUTES

•Make **Black Bean Chilicorn** by adding one 15-ounce can black beans, drained, to the mixture. Or make **Beefy Chilicorn** by adding one pound cooked ground beef, doubling the chili powder, and topping the mixture with one cup of shredded Cheddar cheese.

1 (15¼-ounce) can whole
   kernel corn, drained
1 teaspoon chili powder

1 (14.5-ounce) can Mexican-
   style stewed tomatoes,
   undrained

Combine all ingredients in a saucepan; cook over medium heat until thoroughly heated. Yield: 4 servings.

Corn and Green Chile Casserole

PREP: 2 MINUTES   COOK: 31 MINUTES

1 tablespoon butter or
   margarine
1 (8-ounce) package cream
   cheese, softened
2 (10-ounce) packages frozen
   whole kernel corn, thawed
   and drained

1 (4.5-ounce) can chopped
   green chiles, undrained
¼ teaspoon salt
¼ teaspoon pepper

Melt butter in a heavy saucepan over low heat; add cream cheese, and stir until blended. Stir in corn and remaining ingredients. Spoon into a lightly greased 1-quart baking dish. Cover and bake at 375° for 30 minutes or until thoroughly heated. Yield: 6 servings.

Grilled Eggplant

PREP: 5 MINUTES   GRILL: 10 MINUTES

•For **Eggplant Sandwiches**, add slices of provolone or mozzarella cheese to eggplant slices during the last two minutes of cooking, and serve on firm rolls.

½ teaspoon dried thyme
¼ teaspoon salt
¼ teaspoon dried rosemary,
   crushed
¼ teaspoon pepper

1 medium eggplant, unpeeled
   (about 1¼ pounds)
¼ cup commercial Italian
   salad dressing

Combine first 4 ingredients. Cut eggplant into ½-inch-thick slices. Brush both sides of each slice with dressing, and sprinkle evenly with herb mixture. Grill, covered with grill lid, over medium-hot coals (350° to 400°) 5 minutes on each side or to desired doneness. Yield: 4 servings.

EGGPLANT PARMESAN

Eggplant Parmesan

PREP: 12 MINUTES   **COOK: 45 MINUTES**

1 (1½-pound) eggplant
1 cup shredded refrigerated
   Parmesan cheese
2 cups (8 ounces) shredded
   mozzarella cheese

1½ cups spaghetti sauce or
   marinara sauce

•This recipe also serves
nicely as a meatless entrée
for four. Just add a tossed
salad.

Peel eggplant, if desired, and cut eggplant into ¼-inch-thick slices.
Layer half of eggplant, half of Parmesan cheese, ¾ cup mozzarella,
and half of spaghetti sauce in a lightly greased 11- x 7- x 1½-inch
baking dish. Repeat layers.

Cover and bake at 375° for 40 minutes or until eggplant is tender.
Uncover, top with remaining ½ cup mozzarella cheese, and bake 5 more
minutes or until cheese melts. Yield: 6 servings.

Sparkling Mushrooms

PREP: 5 MINUTES   COOK: 8 MINUTES

1 (8-ounce) package small
  whole mushrooms
2 tablespoons olive oil
½ teaspoon fresh or dried
  rosemary, crushed

⅛ teaspoon salt
⅛ teaspoon pepper
½ cup champagne or
  sparkling wine

•If champagne seems extravagant for a weeknight, try a reasonably priced sparkling wine, such as a Mumm Cuvvee, available in the wine section of grocery stores.

Trim mushroom stems, if desired. Cook mushrooms in oil in a skillet over medium-high heat, stirring constantly, 2 minutes. Add rosemary, salt, and pepper; cook 1 minute. Stir in champagne. Reduce heat; simmer, uncovered, 5 minutes. Yield: 2 servings.

Buttery Green Peas and Mushrooms

PREP: 9 MINUTES   COOK: 6 MINUTES

1 (10-ounce) package frozen
  English peas
1 (4-ounce) can sliced
  mushrooms, drained
1 tablespoon butter or
  margarine

1½ teaspoons dried onion
  flakes
¼ teaspoon salt
¼ teaspoon pepper

Cook peas according to package directions; drain. Add mushrooms and remaining ingredients; cover and let stand 5 minutes. Stir well. Yield: 4 servings.

Microwave Directions: Defrost peas in package at MEDIUM (50% power) 2½ minutes. Place peas in a 1-quart casserole. Cover with heavy-duty plastic wrap; fold back one corner to allow steam to escape. Microwave at HIGH 2 to 3 minutes. Stir in mushrooms and remaining ingredients; cover and microwave at HIGH 1 minute. Let stand 5 minutes. Stir well.

Parmesan Onions

PREP: 7 MINUTES **GRILL: 30 MINUTES**

3 large sweet onions, cut in half crosswise

2 tablespoons butter or margarine

⅓ cup grated Parmesan cheese

½ teaspoon salt

¼ teaspoon pepper

Place each onion half, cut side up, in center of a 12-inch square of heavy-duty aluminum foil. Dot each with butter; sprinkle with cheese, salt, and pepper. Wrap onion halves tightly in foil.

Grill, covered with grill lid, over medium-hot coals (350° to 400°) 20 to 30 minutes or until onion halves are tender. Yield: 6 servings.

•We prefer Vidalias in this recipe. The cheese creates a crusty topping when grilled. If you prefer not to grill, bake foil-wrapped onion halves at 350° for 30 minutes or until tender.

Spinach-Stuffed Peppers

PREP: 2 MINUTES **COOK: 35 MINUTES**

1 (12-ounce) package frozen spinach soufflé, thawed

¼ cup Italian-seasoned breadcrumbs

2 small sweet red peppers, cut in half lengthwise and seeded

Grated Parmesan cheese

Combine spinach soufflé and breadcrumbs; spoon into pepper halves. Place in a shallow baking dish, and sprinkle with cheese. Cover and bake at 350° for 35 minutes. Yield: 4 servings.

Three-Pepper Sauté

PREP: 10 MINUTES   COOK: 8 MINUTES

•This is a very pretty side dish, but sweet peppers can be pricey. Use three green peppers, instead, for a less expensive version.

1 large sweet red pepper
1 large sweet yellow pepper
1 large green pepper
4 green onions, cut into ½-inch pieces
1 clove garlic, minced

2 tablespoons olive oil
1 tablespoon chopped fresh basil
½ teaspoon salt
¼ teaspoon pepper

Seed each pepper, and cut into ¼-inch strips. Cook pepper strips, onions, and garlic in oil in a large skillet over medium-high heat 6 to 8 minutes or until tender, stirring often. Stir in basil, salt, and pepper. Yield: 4 servings.

ITALIAN-SEASONED FRIES

Parmesan-Crusted Potato Wedges

PREP: 8 MINUTES COOK: 30 MINUTES

¼ cup grated Parmesan
　cheese
¼ cup all-purpose flour
1 teaspoon garlic salt

½ teaspoon salt
¼ teaspoon pepper
6 medium potatoes, unpeeled
½ cup butter or margarine

Combine first 5 ingredients in a large heavy-duty, zip-top plastic bag. Cut potatoes lengthwise into fourths; add potato wedges to bag, and shake gently to coat. Set aside.

　Place butter in a 15- x 10- x 1-inch jellyroll pan lined with aluminum foil. Place pan in a 425° oven until butter melts. Spread potato wedges in a single layer in pan, and return to oven. Bake, uncovered, 30 minutes, turning wedges after 15 minutes. Yield: 6 servings.

Italian-Seasoned Fries

PREP: 5 MINUTES COOK: 22 MINUTES

2 large eggs, lightly beaten
3 tablespoons vegetable oil,
　butter, or margarine,
　melted
1 (28-ounce) package frozen
　steak fries

¾ cup Italian-seasoned
　breadcrumbs
¼ cup grated Parmesan
　cheese
1 teaspoon salt

Combine eggs and oil in a large heavy-duty, zip-top plastic bag. Add frozen fries; seal bag, and toss. Combine breadcrumbs and cheese; add to fries, and toss well.

　Place coated fries in a single layer on a lightly greased large baking sheet or jellyroll pan; sprinkle with salt. Bake, uncovered, at 450° for 22 minutes or until browned and crisp. Yield: 8 servings.

•These crusty fries are similar to the "from scratch" version above, but they're made quicker and easier by starting with frozen fries.

•Add one to two teaspoons of your favorite dried herb or other seasoning to the cheese mixture.

Mashed Potato Casserole

PREP: 12 MINUTES   **COOK: 30 MINUTES**

•Tap the bag of frozen potatoes on the countertop, and knead them gently to break apart flakes. This will make them easy to measure without thawing.

3 cups frozen mashed
  potatoes*
1½ cups milk
1 (16-ounce) carton sour
  cream
¼ cup frozen chopped chives

2 tablespoons minced onion
1 tablespoon prepared
  horseradish
1 teaspoon salt
1 teaspoon butter or
  margarine, melted

Prepare potatoes according to package directions, using 1½ cups milk. Add sour cream and next 4 ingredients, stirring well.

Spoon mixture into a lightly greased 2-quart baking dish, and drizzle with butter.

Bake, uncovered, at 350° for 30 minutes or until thoroughly heated. Yield: 8 servings.

*For frozen mashed potatoes, we used Ore-Ida.

Southern-Fried Potatoes

PREP: 6 MINUTES   **COOK: 16 MINUTES**

•This is rustic cooking at its best. Leave the skins on the potatoes, if you'd prefer. They'll fry crispy brown and save you a step, too.

•A cast-iron skillet is an inexpensive investment. Foods cooked in it absorb iron, which will increase the amount of iron you consume.

3 large red potatoes, peeled
  and cut into 1½-inch
  chunks

½ cup vegetable oil
1 small onion, chopped
Salt and pepper to taste

Fry potato chunks in hot oil in a 9- or 10-inch cast-iron skillet over medium-high heat 12 minutes, turning often. Add onion, and cook 5 more minutes. Remove mixture to a serving bowl, using a slotted spoon. Sprinkle with salt and pepper. Yield: 4 servings.

SOUTHERN-FRIED POTATOES

PESTO MASHED POTATOES

CHEDDAR MASHED POTATOES

Creamy Mashed Potatoes

PREP: 4 MINUTES   COOK: 3 MINUTES

•You can substitute an eight-ounce container of plain cream cheese and ⅓ cup sliced green onions for the cream cheese with chives and onion.

1⅓ cups water
½ cup milk
1⅓ cups mashed potato flakes*
¼ teaspoon salt

¼ teaspoon pepper
1 (8-ounce) container cream cheese with chives and onion, softened

Combine water and milk in a microwave-safe bowl; add potato flakes, stirring just until moistened. Microwave, uncovered, at HIGH 3 to 3½ minutes. Add salt, pepper, and cream cheese, stirring until smooth. Serve immediately. Yield: 4 servings.

*For mashed potato flakes, use Hungry Jack or Idaho Spuds.

Variations: For **Mexican Mashed Potatoes,** omit cream cheese; stir in 1 cup (4 ounces) shredded Monterey Jack cheese with peppers.

For **Pesto Mashed Potatoes,** omit cream cheese; stir ¼ to ⅓ cup commercial pesto sauce into hot potatoes.

For **Garlic Mashed Potatoes,** omit cream cheese. Melt 3 tablespoons butter or margarine in a small skillet; add 4 small cloves garlic, crushed. Cook over medium heat, stirring constantly, 1 minute or until garlic is golden. Stir into hot potatoes.

For **Cheddar Mashed Potatoes,** omit cream cheese and, if desired, pepper; increase salt to ½ teaspoon, and add ¼ teaspoon hot sauce. Place prepared potatoes in a lightly greased 1-quart baking dish. Beat ¼ cup whipping cream until stiff peaks form; fold in ¾ cup (3 ounces) shredded sharp Cheddar cheese. Gently spread cheese mixture over potatoes. Bake at 350° for 20 minutes.

Leftover Potato Pancakes

PREP: 10 MINUTES   COOK: 17 MINUTES

1 (16-ounce) package frozen
    whole kernel corn, thawed
½ cup finely chopped onion
½ cup chopped green onions
2 teaspoons vegetable oil
2 cups cooked mashed
    potatoes
½ cup all-purpose flour
2 large eggs, lightly beaten
¾ teaspoon salt
½ teaspoon freshly ground
    pepper
Vegetable cooking spray

•If you have a jar of salsa in the refrigerator, spoon a little over these golden potato patties.

Cook first 3 ingredients in vegetable oil in a large nonstick skillet over medium-high heat, stirring constantly, until vegetables are crisp-tender. Remove from heat.

Combine mashed potatoes, flour, and eggs, stirring well; stir in corn mixture, salt, and pepper.

Coat a large nonstick skillet with cooking spray. Place over medium heat until hot. Drop mixture by one-fourth cupfuls into skillet; cook 2 to 3 minutes on each side or until golden, coating skillet as necessary with additional cooking spray. Serve with salsa. Yield: 18 (2-inch) pancakes.

Ultimate Stuffed Potatoes

PREP: 20 MINUTES · COOK: 31 MINUTES

•Great with burgers or steaks or anything else, stuffed potatoes are a universal favorite. They take a few extra minutes, so if you need a shortcut, prepare them up to the final baking, a day ahead, and chill. Then reheat before serving.

6 slices bacon
4 large baking potatoes
¼ cup butter or margarine
¼ cup whipping cream
1 (8-ounce) carton sour cream
¾ cup (3 ounces) shredded sharp Cheddar cheese
½ cup chopped green onions

3 tablespoons grated Parmesan cheese
½ teaspoon garlic salt
¼ teaspoon pepper
Chopped fresh or frozen chives, thawed

Place bacon on a microwave-safe rack in an 11- x 7- x 1½-inch baking dish; cover with paper towels. Microwave at HIGH 5 to 7 minutes or until bacon is crisp. Drain bacon; crumble and set aside.

Scrub potatoes; prick several times with a fork. Place potatoes 1 inch apart on microwave-safe rack or on paper towels. Microwave at HIGH 14 minutes or until done, turning and rearranging after 5 minutes. Let stand 2 minutes.

Cut potatoes in half lengthwise; carefully scoop out pulp, leaving ¼-inch-thick shells. Combine pulp, butter, and whipping cream in a large bowl; mash until fluffy. Stir in sour cream and next 5 ingredients.

Spoon mixture evenly into potato shells, and place on a baking sheet. Bake at 400° for 10 minutes or until thoroughly heated. Sprinkle with bacon and chives. Yield: 8 servings.

Garlic New Potatoes

PREP: 6 MINUTES · COOK: 13 MINUTES

18 new potatoes, quartered (about 2¾ pounds)
¼ cup butter or margarine
2 cloves garlic, minced

1 tablespoon chopped fresh parsley
¼ teaspoon pepper

Cook potatoes, covered, in boiling salted water to cover 10 minutes or until tender; drain.

Melt butter in a small skillet over medium-high heat; add garlic, and cook, stirring constantly, 3 minutes or until tender. Add parsley and pepper; pour over potatoes, tossing gently to coat. Yield: 6 servings.

Oven-Browned New Potatoes

PREP: 5 MINUTES   COOK: 30 MINUTES

4 to 6 new potatoes, thinly
   sliced
2 tablespoons vegetable oil
1 tablespoon grated Parmesan
   cheese

½ teaspoon salt
¼ teaspoon garlic powder
¼ teaspoon paprika
¼ teaspoon pepper

Place potato slices in a single layer in a 15- x 10- x 1-inch jellyroll pan lined with aluminum foil. Combine oil and remaining 5 ingredients; brush seasoning mixture over potato slices. Bake, uncovered, at 400° for 30 minutes. Yield: 2 servings.

Grilled Tomato Fans

PREP: 11 MINUTES   GRILL: 10 MINUTES

4 firm ripe tomatoes
1 (6-ounce) package
   mozzarella cheese slices
12 large fresh basil leaves
¼ cup olive oil
2 tablespoons chopped fresh
   thyme or 1 teaspoon dried
   thyme

¾ teaspoon dried crushed red
   pepper
3 large cloves garlic, minced

• It's important to use firm tomatoes in this recipe so they'll maintain their shape during grilling.

Turn each tomato on its side. Make 3 vertical cuts in each tomato, cutting to, but not through, bottom.

Cut each slice of cheese into 6 equal pieces. Place 2 pieces of cheese and a basil leaf into each tomato cut. Place each tomato in center of a large square of heavy-duty aluminum foil. Combine oil and remaining 3 ingredients; drizzle over tomatoes. Wrap foil securely around each tomato.

Grill tomatoes, covered with grill lid, over medium-hot coals (350° to 400°) 8 to 10 minutes or just until tomatoes are thoroughly heated and cheese is melted. Unwrap and serve immediately. Yield: 4 servings.

Provençale Tomatoes

2 medium tomatoes, halved crosswise
2 teaspoons Dijon mustard
1/4 teaspoon pepper
1/4 cup Italian-seasoned breadcrumbs
2 teaspoons olive oil

Place tomato halves, cut side up, in a greased baking dish. Spread top of each tomato half with 1/2 teaspoon mustard; sprinkle evenly with pepper and breadcrumbs. Drizzle with oil. Bake at 450° for 10 minutes or until tops are golden. Yield: 4 servings.

Grilled Summer Vegetable Packet

1 large green pepper
4 yellow squash, sliced
2 medium-size firm ripe tomatoes, sliced
1 large sweet onion, thinly sliced
1 large clove garlic, thinly sliced
1 tablespoon chopped fresh rosemary
3/4 teaspoon salt
1/2 teaspoon pepper
1 tablespoon butter or margarine

Slice pepper into 1/2-inch rings; remove and discard seeds and membranes. Place pepper rings, squash, and next 3 ingredients on a large piece of heavy-duty aluminum foil; sprinkle with rosemary, salt, and pepper. Dot with butter. Wrap in foil. Grill, covered with grill lid, over medium coals (300° to 350°) 9 to 10 minutes on each side. Yield: 6 servings.

GARDEN SAUTÉ

Garden Sauté

PREP: **9** MINUTES   COOK: **9** MINUTES

1 tablespoon vegetable oil
2 cloves garlic, crushed
1 small onion, sliced and
   separated into rings
1 small sweet red pepper,
   seeded and cut into strips
½ pound yellow squash,
   sliced

½ pound zucchini, sliced
4 plum tomatoes, chopped
¼ cup fresh basil strips
1 teaspoon lemon pepper
   seasoning
¼ teaspoon salt
¼ cup grated Parmesan
   cheese

•This recipe provides a prime opportunity to show off your summer vegetable garden.

Heat oil in a large nonstick skillet over medium-high heat. Add garlic, onion, and red pepper strips; cook, stirring constantly, 2 minutes. Add yellow squash and zucchini slices; cook, stirring constantly, 5 minutes or until vegetables are crisp-tender.

  Stir in tomato and next 3 ingredients; cook 2 minutes or until thoroughly heated. Remove from heat, and sprinkle with cheese. Serve immediately. Yield: 6 servings.

Summer Squash and Pepper Kabobs

PREP: 10 MINUTES   MARINATE: 1 HOUR

GRILL: 12 MINUTES

2 small yellow squash, cut into 1-inch slices
2 small sweet red peppers, seeded and cut into 1-inch pieces
2 small green peppers, seeded and cut into 1-inch pieces
2 small zucchini, cut into ½-inch slices

1 (8-ounce) bottle Italian salad dressing
2 tablespoons grated Parmesan cheese
½ teaspoon ground red pepper

Combine all ingredients in a large heavy-duty, zip-top plastic bag; seal bag, and toss to coat. Let stand at room temperature 1 hour, turning occasionally.

Remove vegetables from marinade, reserving marinade. Alternate vegetables onto eight 12-inch skewers, leaving ½-inch space between pieces. Grill, covered with grill lid, over medium-hot coals (350° to 400°) 10 to 12 minutes or until tender, turning once and brushing often with reserved marinade. Yield: 4 servings.

Parmesan-Zucchini Sticks

PREP: 12 MINUTES   COOK: 10 MINUTES

• Zucchini "fries" are a refreshing surprise. Serve them with your favorite brand of marinara sauce.

½ cup fine, dry breadcrumbs
½ cup grated Parmesan cheese
3 medium zucchini

1 large egg, lightly beaten
Vegetable oil
½ teaspoon salt

Combine breadcrumbs and cheese. Cut zucchini in half crosswise; cut each half into 8 sticks. Dip zucchini sticks in egg; dredge in breadcrumb mixture.

Pour oil to a depth of 2 inches into a Dutch oven or large heavy saucepan; heat to 375°. Fry zucchini sticks in hot oil just until coating is golden. Drain on a wire rack over paper towels. Sprinkle with salt, and serve immediately. Yield: 6 servings.

Black Beans and Rice

PREP: 10 MINUTES   COOK: 10 MINUTES

1 (4.6-ounce) package
 boil-in-bag long-grain rice
Salt to taste
1 (15.5-ounce) can black
 beans, undrained
1 tablespoon extra spicy
 salt-free herb blend*

⅛ teaspoon pepper
½ cup (2 ounces) shredded
 sharp Cheddar cheese
⅓ cup finely chopped onion
1 medium tomato, chopped

•These cheesy beans can be a side dish or main dish.

Cook rice with salt according to package directions. Combine beans, herb blend, and pepper in a saucepan; bring to a boil over medium heat, stirring constantly. Spoon rice onto a serving platter. Pour bean mixture over rice. Top with cheese, onion, and tomato. Yield: 3 servings.

*For herb blend, we used Mrs. Dash.

PARMESAN-ZUCCHINI
STICKS

Tasty Black-Eyed Peas

PREP: 8 MINUTES   COOK: 10 MINUTES

•For the best flavor, we used canned black-eyed peas packed from fresh shelled peas, rather than from dried peas.

4 slices bacon
1 medium-size green pepper, seeded and chopped
1 medium onion, chopped
2 (15.8-ounce) cans black-eyed peas, drained*

1 (14½-ounce) can Cajun-style stewed tomatoes, undrained and chopped
½ teaspoon salt
¼ teaspoon pepper

Cook bacon in a large skillet until crisp; remove bacon, reserving drippings in skillet. Crumble bacon, and set aside.

Cook green pepper and onion in bacon drippings over medium-high heat, stirring constantly, until tender. Add peas and remaining 3 ingredients to skillet. Cook over low heat until thoroughly heated, stirring often. Sprinkle with bacon. Yield: 6 servings.

*For peas, we used Bush's.

Garden Rice

PREP: 5 MINUTES   COOK: 20 MINUTES

1 tablespoon butter or margarine
2 green onions, sliced
1 small zucchini, chopped (about 1 cup)
½ sweet red pepper, seeded and chopped
½ cup long-grain rice, uncooked

1 tablespoon dried parsley flakes
½ teaspoon chicken bouillon granules
¼ teaspoon salt
1 cup water

Melt butter in a saucepan; add green onions, zucchini, and sweet red pepper. Cook over medium-high heat, stirring constantly, until crisp-tender. Add rice and remaining ingredients; bring to a boil. Cover, reduce heat, and cook 15 minutes or until water is absorbed and rice is tender. Yield: 2 servings.

LEMON COUSCOUS

Lemon Couscous

PREP: 5 MINUTES   COOK: 2 MINUTES

1 cup chicken broth
1 tablespoon grated lemon rind
2 tablespoons fresh lemon juice
1 tablespoon butter or margarine
¼ teaspoon salt

⅔ cup couscous, uncooked
2 tablespoons pecan pieces, toasted
2 tablespoons chopped fresh parsley
1 (2-ounce) jar sliced pimiento, drained

•Move over, rice. Couscous is a tiny grain, gaining popularity on the dinner table because it's so quick to cook. Here, it's enhanced with the zing of lemon rind and freshly squeezed juice.

Combine first 5 ingredients in a saucepan; bring to a boil. Add couscous, stirring well; cover, remove from heat, and let stand 5 minutes. Fluff couscous with a fork. Stir in pecans, parsley, and pimiento. Yield: 3 servings.

Vegetable-Brown Rice Stir-Fry

PREP: 2 MINUTES **COOK: 14 MINUTES**

1 (4½-ounce) package
   boil-in-bag brown and
   wild rice mix
3 tablespoons cashew halves
1 tablespoon peanut or
   vegetable oil
1 (16-ounce) package frozen
   broccoli, carrots, water
   chestnuts, and red peppers

1 tablespoon cornstarch
¾ teaspoon chicken bouillon
   granules
½ teaspoon garlic powder
⅛ teaspoon ground ginger
¾ cup water
1½ tablespoons soy sauce

Prepare rice according to package directions; keep warm.
  Cook cashews in oil in a large skillet over medium-high heat, stirring constantly, until lightly browned; remove from skillet, and set aside.
  Add frozen vegetables to skillet, and cook, stirring constantly, 6 to 8 minutes or until tender.
  Combine cornstarch and next 3 ingredients; stir in water and soy sauce. Add to vegetables in skillet; cook, stirring constantly, 4 minutes or until thickened and bubbly. Stir in cashews, and serve immediately over rice. Yield: 3 servings.

Fettuccine Alfredo

PREP: 5 MINUTES **COOK: 20 MINUTES**

•We give the convenient option of using commercial shredded Parmesan, but if you have a few minutes to grate it fresh, the rich flavor is worth the effort in this classic pasta.

8 ounces dried fettuccine,
   uncooked
½ cup butter
½ cup whipping cream
¾ cup refrigerated shredded
   Parmesan cheese

¼ teaspoon ground white
   pepper
2 tablespoons chopped fresh
   parsley

Cook pasta according to package directions; drain and keep warm.
  Meanwhile, combine butter and whipping cream in a saucepan; cook over medium-low heat until butter melts. Stir in cheese, pepper, and parsley. Pour cheese mixture over hot pasta; toss until pasta is coated. Yield: 4 servings.

Ranch-Style Primavera

PREP: 8 MINUTES COOK: 18 MINUTES

10 ounces dried fettuccine, uncooked

2 cups fresh broccoli flowerets

1½ cups thinly sliced carrot

1 (16-ounce) bottle Ranch-style dressing

1 (6-ounce) package frozen snow pea pods, thawed

1 tablespoon freshly ground pepper

¼ cup grated Parmesan cheese

2 tablespoons chopped fresh parsley

Cook pasta according to package directions, adding broccoli and carrot slices during last 5 minutes of cooking time. Drain.

Warm salad dressing in a large skillet over medium heat. Add pasta mixture, snow peas, and pepper to skillet; toss to coat. Remove from heat; sprinkle with cheese and parsley. Serve immediately. Yield: 8 servings.

RANCH-STYLE PRIMAVERA

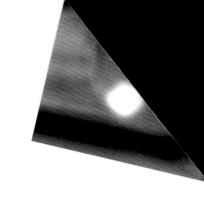

LINGUINE WITH
FRESH TOMATO SAUCE

Linguine with Fresh Tomato Sauce

PREP: 9 MINUTES   **COOK: 11 MINUTES**

1 (12-ounce) package dried
     linguine
4 large tomatoes, chopped
3 tablespoons chopped fresh
     basil
2 cloves garlic, minced
1 tablespoon olive oil

½ teaspoon salt
¼ teaspoon freshly ground
     pepper
1 (2¼-ounce) can sliced ripe
     olives, drained
¾ cup crumbled feta cheese

•Summer-ripened tomatoes make all the difference in this dish.
•Use garlic-and-herb feta for high flavor.

Cook pasta according to package directions.

   Meanwhile, combine tomato and next 5 ingredients. Drain pasta, and place in a large serving bowl. Top with tomato mixture, and sprinkle with olives and cheese. Yield: 6 servings.

Tomato-Jalapeño Pasta

PREP: 15 MINUTES   **COOK: 16 MINUTES**

1 (7-ounce) package dried
     vermicelli
6 cloves garlic, crushed
2 tablespoons olive oil
4 jalapeño peppers, seeded
     and minced

8 plum tomatoes, chopped
½ cup shredded fresh basil
Freshly grated Parmesan
     cheese
½ teaspoon salt
Garnish: fresh basil sprigs

•For maximum heat from the jalapeño peppers, don't seed them.

Cook pasta according to package directions; drain.

   Meanwhile, cook garlic in oil in a large skillet over medium-high heat, stirring constantly, until golden. Add minced pepper, and cook 1 minute. Add tomato; cook 3 minutes or until thoroughly heated, stirring occasionally. Stir in shredded basil. Serve over hot pasta, and sprinkle with cheese and salt. Garnish, if desired. Yield: 4 servings.

Ravioli with Creamy Pesto Sauce

PREP: 1 MINUTE   COOK: 10 MINUTES

• Pine nuts are small blonde kernels that smell like popcorn as you're toasting them. They are, indeed, harvested from pinecones.

1 cup whipping cream
1 (3-ounce) jar pesto sauce
1 (3.5-ounce) jar capers, drained (optional)
2 (9-ounce) packages refrigerated cheese-filled ravioli, uncooked

2 tablespoons pine nuts, toasted

Combine whipping cream and pesto sauce in a saucepan; add capers, if desired. Cook over low heat until thoroughly heated, stirring often.

Meanwhile, cook pasta according to package directions; drain well. Toss pasta with pesto mixture, and sprinkle with pine nuts. Serve immediately. Yield: 4 to 6 servings.

Cheese Tortellini in Tomato Sauce

PREP: 2 MINUTES   COOK: 10 MINUTES

1 (9-ounce) package refrigerated cheese-filled tortellini, uncooked
1 (15-ounce) can chunky Italian-style tomato sauce*

1 jalapeño pepper, seeded and finely chopped
½ cup freshly grated Parmesan cheese

Cook pasta according to package directions; drain.

Meanwhile, combine tomato sauce and pepper in a saucepan; cook over medium heat until thoroughly heated, stirring occasionally. Spoon sauce over pasta; sprinkle with cheese. Yield: 4 servings.

*For tomato sauce, we used Hunt's Ready Tomato Sauce.

PAGE 198

PAGE 190

Fuss-Free Breads

PAGE 186

PAGE 194

NO ONE WILL GUESS YOU TOOK A SHORTCUT FOR CLOUDLIKE
ROLLS, CRUSTY CORNBREADS, AND GARLIC BREADSTICKS.
ALMOST HALF OF THESE RECIPES MAKE GREAT USE OF FOUR
INGREDIENTS OR LESS. SAVE EVEN MORE TIME WITH EASY
EMBELLISHMENTS FOR FRENCH BREAD AND BISCUIT MIXES.

PAGE 189

PAGE 197

Cheddar Biscuits

PREP: 7 MINUTES   COOK: 10 MINUTES

- Sharp Cheddar stirs big flavor into these biscuits, but if you like a more mellow taste, use medium or mild Cheddar.

- To store leftover biscuits, let them cool completely on a wire rack. Place biscuits in an airtight container, and chill overnight.

1 cup biscuit and baking mix
½ cup (2 ounces) shredded
    sharp Cheddar cheese

¼ to ⅓ cup milk

Combine biscuit mix and cheese; add milk, stirring just until dry ingredients are moistened. (Dough will be very soft.) Turn dough out onto a floured surface, and knead lightly 3 or 4 times.

Roll dough to ½-inch thickness; cut into rounds with a 2-inch biscuit cutter. Place biscuits on a lightly greased baking sheet.

Bake at 450° for 10 minutes or until golden. Serve immediately. Yield: 8 biscuits.

Potato Biscuits

PREP: 10 MINUTES   COOK: 12 MINUTES

- Instant potato flakes add to the soft, light texture of these biscuits.

1 (2.1-ounce) package instant
    mashed potato flakes*
    (1 cup)
2 tablespoons butter or
    margarine, cut into pieces

1 teaspoon sugar
1 cup hot water
3 cups biscuit and baking mix
⅓ cup cold water

Combine first 4 ingredients in a large bowl. Add biscuit mix and cold water, stirring just until blended. (Dough will be crumbly.) Turn dough out onto a lightly floured surface, and knead 10 times.

Roll dough to ½-inch thickness on a lightly floured surface; cut with a 2-inch biscuit cutter. Place biscuits on an ungreased baking sheet.

Bake at 450° for 10 to 12 minutes or until biscuits are lightly browned. Yield: 1 dozen.

*For instant potato flakes, we used Hungry Jack.

Quick Biscuits

PREP: 12 MINUTES   COOK: 13 MINUTES

⅔ cup sour cream
⅔ cup club soda

2 tablespoons sugar
4 cups biscuit and baking mix

Combine first 3 ingredients in a large bowl, stirring well. Add biscuit mix, stirring just until dry ingredients are moistened. Turn dough out onto a lightly floured surface, and knead 3 or 4 times.

Shape dough into 12 biscuits (about 1 inch thick). Place 1 biscuit each in centers of two lightly greased 8-inch round cakepans. Arrange remaining biscuits in a circle around center biscuits.

Bake at 450° for 13 minutes or until golden. Yield: 1 dozen.

Sour Cream-Praline Biscuits

PREP: 7 MINUTES   COOK: 18 MINUTES

¾ cup chopped pecans
½ cup firmly packed brown
   sugar
⅓ cup butter or margarine,
   melted

2 cups biscuit and baking mix
1 (8-ounce) carton sour cream

• Try these sweet upside-down biscuits with sliced ham or turkey for dinner.

Combine first 3 ingredients, stirring well. Pour into a lightly greased 9-inch square pan.

Combine biscuit mix and sour cream; stir 30 seconds. Drop batter by ¼ cupfuls over pecan mixture. Bake at 400° for 18 minutes or until biscuits are golden. Invert pan immediately onto a serving platter. Serve immediately. Yield: 9 biscuits.

TINY CREAM CHEESE BISCUITS

Tiny Cream Cheese Biscuits

PREP: 8 MINUTES   COOK: 17 MINUTES

•These little biscuits are so wonderfully buttery that you don't need to grease the muffin pans.

•This is a three-ingredient recipe worth committing to memory. It uses self-rising flour with leavening built in, so most of the measuring is done for you.

1 (8-ounce) package cream cheese, softened

½ cup butter or margarine, softened

1 cup self-rising flour

Beat cream cheese and butter at medium speed of an electric mixer 2 minutes or until creamy. Gradually add flour, beating at low speed just until blended.

  Spoon dough into ungreased miniature (1¾-inch) muffin pans, filling full. Bake at 400° for 15 to 17 minutes or until golden. Serve hot. Yield: 1½ dozen.

Parmesan Toast Wedges

PREP: 3 MINUTES   **COOK: 10 MINUTES**

1 hamburger bun
1 tablespoon olive oil
1 tablespoon grated Parmesan
  cheese
¼ teaspoon dried basil
⅛ teaspoon garlic salt

•Here's the perfect use for leftover hamburger buns.

•This recipe works with hot dog buns, too.

Brush cut sides of bun with oil. Combine cheese, basil, and garlic salt; sprinkle evenly over bun halves. Cut each half into wedges, and place on a baking sheet. Bake at 350° for 10 minutes or until golden. Yield: 2 servings.

Easy Garlic Bread

PREP: 9 MINUTES   **COOK: 25 MINUTES**

½ cup butter or margarine,
  softened
¼ cup grated Parmesan
  cheese
¼ teaspoon dried marjoram
¼ teaspoon dried oregano
2 large cloves garlic, crushed
1 (16-ounce) loaf sliced
  French bread

•Buying a loaf of sliced bread for this recipe cuts your work to a minimum.

•Marjoram tastes similar to oregano; it's just not as commonly used. You'll find them both on the spice aisle.

•You can use ½ teaspoon of just one dried herb, if preferred.

Combine first 5 ingredients; spread between bread slices. Wrap loaf in heavy-duty aluminum foil; place on a baking sheet. Bake at 350° for 20 minutes. Open foil, and bake 5 more minutes or until crisp and golden. Yield: 1 loaf.

Green Onion French Bread

PREP: 7 MINUTES   COOK: 3 MINUTES

¾ cup (3 ounces) shredded
   Cheddar cheese
½ cup mayonnaise
¼ cup butter or margarine,
   softened

¼ cup chopped green onions
¼ teaspoon pepper
1 (16-ounce) loaf unsliced
   French bread

Combine first 5 ingredients, stirring well. Slice bread in half lengthwise. Spread cheese mixture on cut sides of bread. Place bread on an ungreased baking sheet; broil 5½ inches from heat (with electric oven door partially opened) 3 minutes or until cheese topping is bubbly. Yield: 1 loaf.

Mexican Cheese Toast

PREP: 7 MINUTES   COOK: 18 MINUTES

•This deluxe toast is smothered in a Mexican cheese blend. Serve it alongside a tossed salad or black bean chili.

1 (8-ounce) package shredded
   Mexican blend cheese
¾ cup mayonnaise
1½ teaspoons dried parsley
   flakes

⅛ teaspoon garlic powder
1 (16-ounce) loaf unsliced
   French bread

Combine first 4 ingredients, stirring well. Slice bread in half lengthwise. Spread cheese mixture on cut sides of bread. Place bread on an ungreased baking sheet. Bake at 350° for 18 minutes or until cheese melts and bread is lightly browned. Serve immediately. Yield: 1 loaf.

VEGETABLE-BEEF SOUP

VEGGIE-HERB CHEESE TOAST

Veggie-Herb Cheese Toast

PREP: 11 MINUTES   COOK: 4 MINUTES

1 cup (4 ounces) shredded
   mozzarella cheese
¾ cup shredded carrot
¼ cup mayonnaise
½ teaspoon dried Italian
   seasoning

2 green onions, sliced
8 (¾-inch) slices French
   bread

•Flecks of carrot and green onion dot this cheese-covered loaf. Dip a slice into a bowl of Vegetable-Beef Soup (page 126).

•To save some prep time, buy already sliced bread, shredded cheese, and shredded carrots.

Combine first 5 ingredients; set aside.

  Place bread slices on an ungreased baking sheet; broil 5½ inches from heat (with electric oven door partially opened) 2 minutes or until bread is lightly browned. Turn bread slices over, and spread cheese mixture on untoasted sides. Broil 2 more minutes or until topping melts. Serve immediately. Yield: 4 servings.

GREEK BREAD

Greek Bread

PREP: 10 MINUTES   COOK: 15 MINUTES

1 (8-ounce) package cream cheese, softened

2 tablespoons mayonnaise

2 teaspoons Greek seasoning*

1 (16-ounce) loaf unsliced French bread

1 (4-ounce) package tomato-basil or plain feta cheese

1 (2¼-ounce) can sliced ripe olives, drained

½ cup drained, chopped pepperoncini peppers

Combine first 3 ingredients, stirring until smooth. Slice bread loaf in half lengthwise. Spread cream cheese mixture on cut sides of bread. Sprinkle feta cheese, olives, and peppers over cream cheese mixture. Place bread on an ungreased baking sheet. Bake at 375° for 15 minutes or until thoroughly heated. Yield: 1 loaf.

*For Greek seasoning, we used Cavender's. You'll find it on the spice aisle.

Parmesan-Grilled Garlic Bread

PREP: 10 MINUTES   **GRILL: 15 MINUTES**

1 (16-ounce) loaf unsliced
   French bread
½ cup butter or margarine,
   softened
¼ cup grated Parmesan
   cheese

¼ teaspoon pepper
1 clove garlic, crushed
Dash of ground red pepper

Slice bread loaf diagonally into 1-inch slices. Combine butter and remaining 4 ingredients; spread between bread slices. Wrap bread in heavy-duty aluminum foil. Grill, covered with grill lid, over medium-hot coals (350° to 400°) 15 minutes, turning once. Yield: 1 loaf.

Italian Cheese Breadsticks

PREP: 5 MINUTES   **COOK: 12 MINUTES**

1 (11-ounce) can refrigerated
   breadsticks
1 to 2 tablespoons olive oil
1½ teaspoons garlic powder

1 teaspoon dried Italian
   seasoning
1 cup (4 ounces) shredded
   mozzarella cheese

•Dip these pizza-flavored sticks into your favorite brand of marinara sauce.

Unroll breadstick dough; twist breadsticks, and place 1 inch apart on a lightly greased aluminum foil-lined baking sheet. Brush breadsticks with oil. Combine garlic powder and Italian seasoning; sprinkle over breadsticks. Bake at 400° for 9 to 10 minutes or until golden. Sprinkle with cheese; bake 1 to 2 more minutes or until cheese melts. Serve immediately. Yield: 8 breadsticks.

Southwest Seasoned Breadsticks

PREP: 16 MINUTES
COOK: 16 MINUTES PER BAKING SHEET

2½ tablespoons butter or margarine, melted
1 teaspoon chili powder

½ teaspoon ground cumin
1 (11-ounce) can refrigerated breadsticks

Combine first 3 ingredients, stirring well. Unroll breadstick dough onto a large cutting board; brush dough with butter mixture. Cut dough in half crosswise; separate dough into 16 pieces.

  Stretch each piece of dough slightly, and twist ends in opposite directions 3 or 4 times. Place 1 inch apart on ungreased baking sheets, pressing ends of dough securely onto baking sheets. Bake at 350° for 15 to 16 minutes or until golden. Yield: 16 breadsticks.

Dijon Biscuit Twists

PREP: 10 MINUTES   COOK: 10 MINUTES

¼ cup grated Parmesan cheese
1½ tablespoons butter or margarine, softened or melted

½ teaspoon Dijon mustard
1 (5-ounce) can refrigerated buttermilk biscuits

Combine first 3 ingredients, stirring well. Roll each biscuit into a 5- x 2-inch rectangle; spread 2 teaspoons cheese mixture over each rectangle. Cut in half lengthwise. Twist each strip 3 times, and place on a lightly greased baking sheet. Bake at 400° for 8 to 10 minutes or until golden. Yield: 10 twists.

Green Chile Cornbread

PREP: 5 MINUTES   COOK: 20 MINUTES

2 (7½-ounce) packages corn muffin mix
1 (8½-ounce) can cream-style corn
1 (4.5-ounce) can chopped green chiles, drained
1 cup (4 ounces) shredded Cheddar cheese
½ cup plain yogurt
¼ cup milk
2 large eggs, lightly beaten

Combine all ingredients, stirring just until moistened. Pour batter into a lightly greased 13- x 9- x 2-inch pan. Bake at 450° for 20 minutes or until golden. Yield: 15 servings.

•Cream-style corn provides a slight sweetness to this pan of crumbly goodness.

Sour Cream Cornbread

PREP: 3 MINUTES   COOK: 25 MINUTES

2 tablespoons shortening
1 cup self-rising cornmeal
1 (8½-ounce) can cream-style corn
1 (8-ounce) carton sour cream
¼ cup vegetable oil
3 large eggs, lightly beaten

Heat shortening in an 8-inch cast-iron skillet at 425° for 5 minutes or until skillet is almost smoking.

  Meanwhile, combine cornmeal and remaining ingredients, stirring just until moistened. Remove skillet from oven; spoon batter into hot skillet. Bake at 425° for 20 minutes or until golden. Yield: 6 servings.

•Self-rising cornmeal has leavening blended in the bag with the cornmeal.

•Listen for the sizzle when you spoon this batter into the hot black skillet with melted shortening. This step is what gives cornbread a crisp edge.

Golden Cornbread Sticks

PREP: 8 MINUTES   **COOK: 25 MINUTES**

•Dunk these ridged corn-sticks in a bowl of hot pinto beans.

2 cups self-rising cornmeal
¼ teaspoon baking soda
2 large eggs, lightly beaten
1 (10¾-ounce) can condensed golden corn soup, undiluted, or 1 (11-ounce) can corn chowder

1½ cups (6 ounces) shredded Cheddar cheese
1 cup buttermilk
¼ cup vegetable oil
1 tablespoon chopped green chiles (from a can)
Vegetable cooking spray

Heat cast-iron corn stick pans at 450° for 5 minutes or until very hot.

Meanwhile, combine cornmeal and baking soda in a large bowl; make a well in center of mixture. Combine eggs and next 5 ingredients; add to cornmeal mixture, stirring just until dry ingredients are moistened.

Remove pans from oven, and coat with cooking spray. Spoon batter into hot pans. Bake at 375° for 18 to 20 minutes or until cornbread sticks are browned. Remove from pans, and let cool slightly on a wire rack. Yield: 2 dozen.

GOLDEN
CORNBREAD
STICKS

Onion Supper Bread

PREP: 8 MINUTES   COOK: 20 MINUTES

1 tablespoon butter or
    margarine
½ cup chopped onion
1 (6-ounce) package
    cornbread mix*

⅔ cup sour cream
1 large egg, lightly beaten
⅓ cup shredded sharp
    Cheddar cheese

Melt butter in a skillet over medium heat; add onion, and cook, stirring constantly, until tender.

Combine cornbread mix, sour cream, and beaten egg, stirring well. Spoon batter into a lightly greased 8-inch square pan; sprinkle with onion and cheese. Bake at 400° for 20 minutes or until lightly browned. Yield: 9 servings.

*For cornbread mix, we used Martha White.

Italian Flatbread

PREP: 16 MINUTES   COOK: 15 MINUTES

1 (32-ounce) package frozen
    bread dough loaves,
    thawed
2 tablespoons olive oil

½ cup freshly grated
    Parmesan cheese
2 teaspoons dried basil
¾ teaspoon garlic powder

• Freeze flatbread rounds to use later as personal-size pizza crusts. Just thaw, add toppings, and bake at 450° for 6 to 8 minutes.

Divide each loaf into 3 portions. Roll each portion into a 6½-inch circle, and place on a lightly greased baking sheet. Brush circles with oil, and sprinkle with cheese, basil, and garlic powder.

Bake at 375° for 10 minutes. Prick several times with a fork. Bake 5 more minutes or until golden. Cool slightly on baking sheet. Cut each round into 4 wedges. Yield: 12 servings.

Italian Pita Wedges

PREP: 10 MINUTES   COOK: 14 MINUTES

•Give these toasted triangles a minute to cool and crisp up before you start to nibble on them.

2 (6- or 8-inch) whole wheat or white pita bread rounds
¼ cup commercial Italian salad dressing

2 cloves garlic, crushed, or ½ teaspoon garlic powder

Separate each pita bread into 2 rounds; cut each round into 6 wedges to make 24 triangles. Combine dressing and garlic; brush over rough side of each triangle. Place, dressing side up, on an ungreased baking sheet. Bake at 350° for 12 to 14 minutes or until golden. Let cool slightly. Yield: 2 dozen.

Cream Cheese Crescents

PREP: 5 MINUTES   COOK: 11 MINUTES

•You can use any flavor of cream cheese in these rolls.

1 (8-ounce) package refrigerated crescent dinner rolls

¼ cup cream cheese with chives, softened

Unroll crescent dough; spread cream cheese over 1 side. Separate dough into 8 triangles. Roll up each triangle, beginning at wide end. Place rolls, point side down, on an ungreased baking sheet. Bake at 375° for 11 minutes or until golden. Yield: 8 rolls.

Mayonnaise Rolls

PREP: 8 MINUTES   COOK: 15 MINUTES

1 cup self-rising flour
½ cup milk

3 tablespoons mayonnaise
¾ teaspoon sugar

Combine all ingredients in a bowl, stirring just until dry ingredients are moistened. Spoon batter into greased muffin pans, filling three-fourths full. Bake at 425° for 15 minutes. Yield: ½ dozen.

SESAME KNOTS

Sesame Knots

PREP: 5 MINUTES   **COOK: 15 MINUTES**

1 (11-ounce) can refrigerated
   breadsticks
2 tablespoons butter or
   margarine, melted

1 teaspoon sesame seeds

Separate dough, and loosely tie each piece of dough into a knot;
place 1 inch apart on an ungreased baking sheet. Brush with butter,
and sprinkle with sesame seeds. Bake at 350° for 15 minutes or until
golden. Yield: 8 servings.

Mustard 'n' Cheddar Pretzel Rolls

PREP: 30 MINUTES   COOK: 14 MINUTES

- •Look for kosher salt on the same grocery aisle as table salt. Its crystals are bigger, so each bite of bread is briskly salty.

- •Kitchen shears make quick work of snipping this dough into 18 pieces.

- •Squirt these salty topped pretzel rolls with mustard, and serve them with a salad.

1 (16-ounce) package hot roll mix with yeast packet
¾ teaspoon dry mustard
1½ cups (6 ounces) shredded sharp Cheddar cheese
1 cup hot water (120° to 130°)

1 large egg, lightly beaten
2 tablespoons butter or margarine, melted
1 large egg, lightly beaten
Kosher salt

Combine hot roll mix, yeast packet, mustard, and cheese; add hot water, 1 egg, and butter, stirring until blended. Turn dough out onto a lightly floured surface, and knead 5 minutes or until smooth. Cover and let rest 5 minutes.

Cut dough into 18 pieces. Roll each piece of dough on a lightly floured surface into a 14-inch rope; twist into a pretzel shape. Place on lightly greased baking sheets. Brush with remaining egg, and sprinkle with salt. Bake at 400° for 14 minutes or until golden. Serve warm. Yield: 18 rolls.

MUSTARD 'N' CHEDDAR
PRETZEL ROLLS

PARMESAN BREAD

Parmesan Bread

PREP: 6 MINUTES   COOK: 2 HOURS AND 40 MINUTES

1 cup water
1 large egg, lightly beaten
2 tablespoons butter or
   margarine, softened
3 cups bread flour
½ cup grated Parmesan
   cheese

2 tablespoons sugar
2 teaspoons dried onion flakes
1½ teaspoons garlic salt
1 package rapid-rise yeast

•This recipe works well using the large loaf setting.

Combine all ingredients in bread machine according to manufacturer's instructions. Process on rapid bake cycle with light crust setting. Remove from pan, and let cool on a wire rack. Yield: one 7-inch loaf.

Honey-Oat Bread

PREP: 7 MINUTES   DELAY: UP TO 13 HOURS
COOK: 2 HOURS AND 40 MINUTES

•We tested this recipe using both 1- and 1½-pound loaf settings. Both received favorable comments.

•A bread machine is a convenient tool that you'll be hooked on once you've tried it. The delayed setting allows you to plan ahead and have fresh baked bread ready with no attention for up to 13 hours before turning the bread out.

1   cup water
¼   cup honey
¼   cup butter or margarine,
      softened
1¼ cups whole wheat flour
1   cup bread flour
½   cup unprocessed oat bran
      or quick-cooking oats,
      uncooked

1   teaspoon salt
1   package rapid-rise yeast or
      2 teaspoons bread machine
      yeast*

Combine all ingredients in bread machine according to manufacturer's instructions. Process in delayed bake cycle, using light crust setting, if available. Remove from pan, and let cool on a wire rack. Yield: one 7-inch loaf.

Variation: You can make egg-enriched bread from this recipe if you're going to bake it immediately after combining ingredients. Just decrease butter to 2 tablespoons, add 1 large egg, and process in regular or rapid bake cycle.

*For bread machine yeast, we used Fleischmann's. Find it in a jar on the aisle with yeast packets and flour.

PAGE 202

PAGE 222

Desserts In A Flash

PAGE 228

PAGE 212

MAKE DESSERT SIMPLE, MAKE IT FAST, AND MAKE IT FUN WITH THESE RECIPES. HALF OF THEM BOAST FIVE OR FEWER INGREDIENTS. YOU'LL BE SURPRISED THAT CAKES AND PIES CAN LOOK SO GOOD WITH SO LITTLE EFFORT.

PAGE 226

PAGE 210

Praline Grahams

PREP: 5 MINUTES COOK: 17 MINUTES

- •This is a delicious cross between a bar cookie and candy. It's an easy and excellent dress-up for any flavor graham cracker— regular, chocolate, or cinnamon.
- •Use margarine instead of butter for best results with the syrupy coating.

12 whole regular graham crackers or chocolate graham crackers*

¾ cup margarine
½ cup sugar
1 cup chopped pecans

Break graham crackers in half. Arrange graham cracker squares with edges touching in an ungreased 15- x 10- x 1-inch jellyroll pan. Set aside.

Melt margarine in a saucepan over medium heat; stir in sugar and pecans. Bring to a boil, stirring constantly. Cook 5 minutes, stirring often. Working quickly, spread syrupy mixture evenly over graham crackers. Bake at 300° for 12 minutes. Remove from pan, and let cool on a wire rack. Yield: 2 dozen.

*For graham crackers, we used Nabisco HoneyMaid. The number of graham crackers per package varies from 10 to 12 depending on the brand. No matter which brand you buy, you'll need at least one package from a box for this recipe.

PRALINE GRAHAMS

Chocolate-Oatmeal Cookies

PREP: 19 MINUTES
COOK: 10 MINUTES PER BAKING SHEET

1 cup (6 ounces) semisweet
   chocolate morsels, divided
1 (22.3-ounce) package sugar
   cookie mix
1 cup quick-cooking oats,
   uncooked

⅓ cup vegetable oil
1 teaspoon water
1 teaspoon vanilla extract
2 large eggs, lightly beaten

•For these chocolaty drops, you get a head start with the dough by using sugar cookie mix.

Melt ½ cup chocolate morsels in a saucepan over low heat, stirring often. Combine melted chocolate, sugar cookie mix, and remaining 5 ingredients in a large bowl, stirring until well blended. Stir in remaining ½ cup chocolate morsels.

  Drop dough by heaping teaspoonfuls 1 inch apart onto lightly greased baking sheets. Bake at 350° for 10 minutes. Let cool slightly; remove to wire racks, and let cool completely. Yield: 5½ dozen.

Polka Dots

PREP: 5 MINUTES
COOK: 8 MINUTES PER BAKING SHEET

1 (21.2-ounce) package fudge
   brownie mix*
½ cup vegetable oil

2 large eggs, lightly beaten
1 cup white chocolate morsels
   or vanilla milk morsels

•Substitute butterscotch morsels for a different flavor Polka Dot.

Combine first 3 ingredients, stirring well. Stir in morsels. Drop dough by rounded teaspoonfuls about 2 inches apart onto ungreased baking sheets. Bake at 350° for 8 minutes. Let cool 2 minutes; remove to wire racks, and let cool completely. Yield: 4 dozen.

*For brownie mix, we used Betty Crocker Fudge Brownie Mix.

Chocolate Macaroons

PREP: 10 MINUTES

COOK: 12 MINUTES PER BAKING SHEET

•Coconut and almond are flavors common to chewy macaroon cookies. No electric mixer's required in this chocolate version— just stir with a spoon.

1 cup sweetened condensed milk
½ cup all-purpose flour
½ teaspoon almond extract or vanilla extract

1 (7-ounce) can flaked coconut
1 (3.9-ounce) package chocolate instant pudding mix

Combine all ingredients, stirring well. Drop by rounded teaspoonfuls onto lightly greased baking sheets. Bake at 325° for 10 to 12 minutes. Remove to wire racks, and let cool. Yield: 3½ dozen.

Toffee Crunch Cookies

PREP: 15 MINUTES

COOK: 12 MINUTES PER BAKING SHEET

•Looking for the best dessert stir-ins? Almond brickle chips are second only to semisweet morsels. They sprinkle on toffee flavor quicker than you can chop a candy bar.

•Look for bags of brickle chips near chocolate morsels, baking squares, and coconut on the baking aisle.

½ cup butter or margarine, softened
1 (18.25-ounce) package yellow cake mix with pudding
2 large eggs

1 tablespoon water
½ cup chopped pecans
1 (7.5-ounce) package almond brickle chips

Beat butter at medium speed of an electric mixer until creamy; add cake mix, eggs, and water, beating until blended. Stir in pecans and brickle chips. Drop dough by tablespoonfuls onto ungreased baking sheets.

Bake at 350° for 10 to 12 minutes or until edges are browned. (Top will look moist.) Let cool slightly. Remove to wire racks, and let cool. Yield: 4 dozen.

See photo on page 213.

Brownie Chip Cookies

PREP: 11 MINUTES

COOK: 8 MINUTES PER BAKING SHEET

1 (23.7-ounce) package double
    fudge brownie mix*
1/3 cup vegetable oil
2 large eggs, lightly beaten

1 cup (6 ounces) semisweet
    chocolate morsels
1/2 cup chopped pecans

•You can freeze these cookies up to six months.

Combine first 3 ingredients in a large bowl, stirring well. Stir in chocolate morsels and pecans. Drop dough by rounded teaspoonfuls onto lightly greased baking sheets. Bake at 350° for 8 minutes. Remove to wire racks, and let cool completely. Yield: about 6 dozen.

*For brownie mix, we used Duncan Hines Double Fudge Brownie Mix (with fudge packet).

Rich Brownies

PREP: 5 MINUTES   COOK: 28 MINUTES

1 (10¼-ounce) package fudge
    brownie mix*
1/2 cup miniature
    marshmallows

1/2 cup semisweet chocolate
    morsels
1/2 cup chopped pecans

•Rich, indeed. These firm brownies come out of the pan easily.
•If you like brownies to be gooey, bake these just 24 minutes; plan to chill them to make cutting easy.

Prepare brownie mix batter according to package directions, folding marshmallows, chocolate morsels, and pecans into batter. Spread batter evenly into a greased 8-inch square pan. Bake at 350° for 28 minutes. Let cool completely in pan on a wire rack; cut into squares. Yield: 16 brownies.

*For brownie mix, we used Gold Medal.

GOOEY TURTLE BARS

Gooey Turtle Bars

PREP: 8 MINUTES   COOK: 15 MINUTES
CHILL: 30 MINUTES

•No bowls needed. Combine crust ingredients right in the pan; then sprinkle and drizzle on the toppings. Cleanup is easy with this recipe.

2 cups graham cracker
   crumbs or vanilla wafer
   crumbs
½ cup butter or margarine,
   melted

2 cups (12 ounces) semisweet
   chocolate morsels
1 cup pecan pieces
1 (12-ounce) jar caramel
   topping

Combine crumbs and butter in an ungreased 13- x 9- x 2-inch pan; stir and press firmly into bottom of pan. Sprinkle with chocolate morsels and pecans.

  Remove lid from caramel topping; microwave at HIGH 1 to 1½ minutes or until hot, stirring after 30 seconds. Drizzle over pecans. Bake at 350° for 15 minutes or until morsels melt; let cool in pan on a wire rack. Chill at least 30 minutes; cut into bars. Yield: 2 dozen.

Peanut Butter Bars

PREP: 7 MINUTES   COOK: 25 MINUTES

½ cup quick-cooking oats, uncooked
⅓ cup self-rising flour
½ cup butter-flavored shortening, melted
1 teaspoon vanilla extract
¼ teaspoon salt
2 large eggs, lightly beaten
1 (14-ounce) can sweetened condensed milk
1 (12-ounce) jar chunky peanut butter

Combine all ingredients in a large bowl, stirring just until blended. Spread mixture into a lightly greased 13- x 9- x 2-inch pan. Bake at 350° for 20 to 25 minutes or until a wooden pick inserted in center comes out clean. Let cool in pan. Cut into bars. Yield: 2 dozen.

• A can and a jar from the pantry are key components in this cakelike brownie. It makes a great not-so-sweet snack.

Canary Lemon Cake

PREP: 11 MINUTES   COOK: 35 MINUTES

1 (18.25-ounce) package lemon supreme cake mix
1 (3.4-ounce) package lemon instant pudding mix
½ cup water
½ cup vegetable oil
4 large eggs
¾ cup lemon juice, divided
2 cups sifted powdered sugar

Combine first 5 ingredients; add ½ cup lemon juice, and beat 2 minutes at medium speed of an electric mixer. Pour batter into a greased and floured 13- x 9- x 2-inch pan. Bake at 350° for 35 minutes or until a wooden pick inserted in center comes out clean. Let cool in pan on a wire rack.

Combine remaining ¼ cup lemon juice and powdered sugar, stirring well; drizzle over cake. Cut into squares. Yield: 15 to 18 servings.

Gingerbread with Lemon Sauce

PREP: 12 MINUTES   COOK: 45 MINUTES

1 (14.5-ounce) package
  gingerbread mix*
1 cup water
½ cup sugar
1½ tablespoons cornstarch

Pinch of salt
2 tablespoons butter or
  margarine
⅓ cup lemon juice

Prepare and bake gingerbread according to package directions.
  Meanwhile, combine water and next 3 ingredients in a saucepan, stirring until smooth. Cook over medium heat, stirring constantly, until thick and bubbly. Remove from heat; add butter and lemon juice. Stir until butter melts. Let cool slightly.
  Prick top of warm gingerbread with a fork; drizzle with ½ cup lemon sauce. Cut into squares; serve with remaining sauce. Yield: 9 servings.

*For gingerbread mix, we used Betty Crocker.

Cranberry-Orange Coffee Cake

PREP: 11 MINUTES   COOK: 25 MINUTES

• This coffee cake's as good for dessert as it is for breakfast, especially if you top it with ice cream.

• Look for plastic tubs of crushed fruit on the canned fruit aisle.

½ cup chopped pecans
¼ cup firmly packed brown
  sugar
¼ teaspoon ground cinnamon
2 cups biscuit and baking mix
2 tablespoons sugar

⅔ cup milk
1 large egg, lightly beaten
½ (12-ounce) tub cranberry-
  orange crushed fruit
Glaze

Combine first 3 ingredients, stirring well. Combine biscuit mix and next 3 ingredients, stirring well. Pour batter into a greased 9-inch square pan. Sprinkle pecan mixture over batter; spoon crushed fruit evenly over pecan mixture. Bake at 400° for 22 to 25 minutes or until a wooden pick inserted in center comes out clean. Drizzle Glaze over warm cake. Yield: one 9-inch coffee cake.

Glaze

1 cup sifted powdered sugar
2 tablespoons milk

½ teaspoon vanilla extract

Combine all ingredients, stirring well. Yield: about ⅓ cup.

Orange Angel Food Cake

PREP: 5 MINUTES   COOK: 45 MINUTES

1 (16-ounce) package angel
  food cake mix*
1 cup water

⅓ cup orange juice
1 teaspoon orange extract or
  flavoring

•In this recipe, the ungreased pan enables the airy batter to climb high and cling to the pan's sides as it bakes.

Prepare cake mix according to package directions, using 1 cup water and ⅓ cup orange juice instead of the liquid called for on the package. Stir in orange extract. Spoon batter into an ungreased 10-inch tube pan.

Bake at 350° on lowest oven rack for 40 to 45 minutes or until cake springs back when lightly touched. Invert pan over the neck of a glass bottle; let cool completely. Loosen cake from sides of pan, and remove from pan. Yield: one 10-inch cake.

*For angel food cake mix, we used Duncan Hines.

Variations:

For **Lemon Angel Food Cake,** omit orange juice and extract, and substitute ¼ cup frozen lemon juice concentrate, thawed, and 2 teaspoons grated lemon rind.

For **Peppermint Angel Food Cake,** omit water, orange juice, and extract. Prepare cake mix according to package directions, stirring 5 hard peppermint candies, crushed, and ¼ teaspoon peppermint extract into batter.

For **Chocolate Angel Food Cake,** omit water, orange juice, and extract. Combine cake mix and ¼ cup sifted cocoa. Prepare cake according to package directions.

For **Coconut Angel Food Cake,** omit water, orange juice, and extract. Prepare cake mix according to package directions, folding ½ cup flaked coconut, toasted, and ¼ teaspoon coconut extract into batter.

Mocha Brownie Cake

PREP: 15 MINUTES   COOK: 25 MINUTES

CHILL: 1 TO 2 HOURS

• You'll get the most volume from whipping cream if you chill or freeze the mixing bowl and beaters 15 minutes beforehand.

• Chilling this dessert gives the coffee-cream filling time to set, and it makes the cake easier to slice and serve.

Vegetable cooking spray
1 (21-ounce) package chewy fudge brownie mix*
⅓ cup water
¼ cup vegetable oil
2 large eggs, lightly beaten

½ cup chopped pecans
1½ cups whipping cream
1 tablespoon instant coffee granules
¼ cup sifted powdered sugar
Garnish: chocolate shavings

Coat two 8-inch cakepans with cooking spray; line pans with wax paper, and coat with cooking spray.

Combine brownie mix and next 3 ingredients; stir in pecans. Spread batter evenly into prepared pans. Bake at 350° for 23 to 25 minutes. Let cool in pans on wire racks 5 minutes; invert onto wire racks. Carefully remove wax paper, and let cake layers cool completely on wire racks.

Combine whipping cream and coffee granules, stirring well. Beat at medium speed of an electric mixer until foamy; gradually add powdered sugar, beating until stiff peaks form. Spread whipped cream mixture between layers and on top and sides of cake. Cover and chill 1 to 2 hours. Garnish, if desired. Yield: one 2-layer cake.

*For brownie mix, we used Duncan Hines Family-Style Fudge Brownie Mix.

MOCHA BROWNIE CAKE

Triple-Chocolate Bundt Cake

PREP: 12 MINUTES   COOK: 55 MINUTES

1 (18.25-ounce) package
   devil's food cake mix with
   pudding
1 (5.9-ounce) package
   chocolate instant pudding
   mix
1¼ cups water

½ cup vegetable oil
4 large eggs
3 cups (18 ounces) semisweet
   chocolate morsels, divided
½ cup whipping cream
Garnish: pecan halves

•Yes, this luscious, seven-ingredient dessert starts with a cake mix and instant pudding.

Combine first 5 ingredients in a large mixing bowl; beat at medium speed of an electric mixer 2 minutes. Stir in 2 cups chocolate morsels. Pour batter into a greased and floured 12-cup Bundt pan.

Bake at 350° for 50 to 55 minutes or until cake springs back when lightly touched. (A wooden pick inserted in center may not come out clean.) Let cool in pan on a wire rack 10 minutes; remove from pan, and let cool completely on wire rack.

Combine remaining 1 cup chocolate morsels and whipping cream in a heavy saucepan; cook over medium heat, stirring constantly, just until morsels melt. Let stand 15 minutes; drizzle chocolate glaze over cake. Garnish, if desired. Let cake stand 1 hour before serving. Yield: one 10-inch cake.

Cheesecake with Baked Cranberry Sauce

PREP: 3 MINUTES   COOK: 25 MINUTES

1 cup fresh or frozen
   cranberries
½ cup sugar
½ cup orange marmalade
¼ cup coarsely chopped
   walnuts, toasted

2½ teaspoons lemon juice
Dash of ground cinnamon
1 (1-pound 7½-ounce) frozen
   French cheesecake,
   thawed*

•You can freeze cranberries up to one year, and there's no need to thaw them before baking.

Combine first 6 ingredients in a greased 1-quart baking dish. Cover and bake at 350° for 25 minutes. Let cool. Serve chilled or at room temperature over cheesecake. Yield: 6 servings.

*For cheesecake, we used Sara Lee.

Easy Brickle Cake

PREP: 14 MINUTES   COOK: 45 MINUTES

•To use a 10-inch tube pan, combine cake mix and next four ingredients; fold in brickle chips. Spoon batter into greased and floured pan. Combine chopped pecans, coconut, and butter; sprinkle mixture over batter in pan. Bake at 350° for 55 minutes. Let cool, and glaze as directed.

½ cup chopped pecans
½ cup flaked coconut
2 tablespoons butter or margarine, melted
1 (18.25-ounce) package yellow or white cake mix with pudding*
1 (8-ounce) carton sour cream
¼ cup water
2 tablespoons vegetable oil
4 large eggs
1 (7.5-ounce) package almond brickle chips
1 cup sifted powdered sugar
1½ tablespoons milk

Combine first 3 ingredients; spread in bottom of a greased and floured 12-cup Bundt pan. Set aside.

Combine cake mix and next 4 ingredients in a large mixing bowl; beat at medium speed of an electric mixer 2 minutes. Fold in brickle chips. Spoon batter into prepared pan.

Bake at 350° for 45 minutes or until a wooden pick inserted in center comes out clean. Let cool in pan 10 minutes; remove from pan, and invert onto a serving plate. Combine powdered sugar and milk; drizzle over warm cake. Yield: one 10-inch cake.

*For cake mix, we used Betty Crocker Supermoist with Pudding.

EASY BRICKLE CAKE

TOFFEE CRUNCH
COOKIES

Marbled Chocolate Bundt Cake

PREP: 14 MINUTES   COOK: 45 MINUTES

•For **Marbled Chocolate Cupcakes,** spoon batter into muffin pans lined with paper baking cups, filling each two-thirds full. Spoon two teaspoons cream cheese mixture into center of each cupcake. Bake at 350° for 25 minutes. Remove from pans; let cool on wire racks. Yield: 30 cupcakes.

1 (18.25-ounce) package devil's food cake mix without pudding
1 teaspoon vanilla extract
1 (8-ounce) package cream cheese, softened
⅓ cup sugar
1 large egg
1 cup (6 ounces) semisweet chocolate morsels

Prepare cake mix batter according to package directions; stir in vanilla. Pour batter into a greased and floured 12-cup Bundt pan; set aside.

Beat cream cheese and sugar at medium speed of an electric mixer until fluffy. Add egg, beating well; stir in chocolate morsels. Spoon cream cheese mixture into center of batter, leaving a border around outer edge. Gently swirl batter with a knife to create a marbled effect.

Bake at 350° for 45 minutes. Let cool in pan on a wire rack 10 to 15 minutes; remove from pan, and let cool completely. Yield: one 10-inch cake.

Fruity Ice Cream Cake

PREP: 10 MINUTES   FREEZE: 8 HOURS

•This cake's unique texture evolves as you stir cake and ice cream together and freeze them. It's a refreshing summertime dessert.

½ gallon vanilla ice cream, softened
1 (14- or 16-ounce) angel food cake, torn into bite-size pieces
1 (10-ounce) package frozen strawberries, thawed
1 (8-ounce) can unsweetened crushed pineapple, undrained
⅓ cup chopped pecans or walnuts, toasted
1 cup frozen whipped topping, thawed
Chocolate syrup (optional)

Combine first 5 ingredients in a large bowl; fold in whipped topping. Spoon mixture into an ungreased 10-inch tube pan. Cover and freeze 8 hours. Remove cake from pan, and slice with a warm knife. Serve with chocolate syrup, if desired. Yield: 16 servings.

Fudge Spoon Pie

PREP: 10 MINUTES   COOK: 22 MINUTES

½ cup butter or margarine
1 (1-ounce) square
   unsweetened chocolate
1 cup sugar

½ cup all-purpose flour
1 teaspoon vanilla extract
2 large eggs, lightly beaten
Ice cream

•This dessert is too rich and gooey to slice like a pie—spoon it out like a cobbler, and top it with your favorite ice cream.

Melt butter and chocolate in a saucepan over low heat, stirring often; remove from heat. Stir in sugar and next 3 ingredients. Pour batter into a greased 8-inch square pan. Bake at 325° for 22 minutes (do not overbake). Serve warm with ice cream. Yield: 9 servings.

FUDGE SPOON PIE

Apple Pie with Caramel-Raisin Sauce

PREP: 6 MINUTES   COOK: 1 HOUR

• This sugary golden sauce makes about 1½ cups. Serve it over ice cream, waffles, or pound cake. Make it using golden raisins, if that's what's in your pantry.

1 (37-ounce) frozen double-crust apple pie*
3 tablespoons butter or margarine
½ cup firmly packed brown sugar
½ cup whipping cream
½ cup raisins
1 teaspoon vanilla extract

Bake pie according to package directions.

  Meanwhile, melt butter in a saucepan. Stir in brown sugar and whipping cream. Cook over medium-low heat, stirring until sugar dissolves (about 10 minutes). Remove from heat; stir in raisins and vanilla. Serve over hot apple pie. Yield: 9 servings.

*For apple pie, we used Sara Lee.

Pecan Pie with Praline Cream

PREP: 4 MINUTES   COOK: 15 MINUTES

• Find praline liqueur at the liquor store. Substitute commercial caramel ice cream topping, if you'd prefer. It'll be a little thicker.

• There are several brands of commercial pecan pies to choose from in the freezer case. They may vary in size slightly, but any one you pick will be enhanced by this rich cream topping and will serve six easily.

1 (32-ounce) frozen pecan pie*
½ cup whipping cream
1 teaspoon praline liqueur or Kahlúa
½ teaspoon vanilla extract
2 tablespoons powdered sugar
¼ cup plus 2 tablespoons praline liqueur or Kahlúa, divided

Bake pie according to package directions.

  Meanwhile, combine whipping cream, 1 teaspoon liqueur, and vanilla in a small mixing bowl; beat at medium speed of an electric mixer until foamy. Add powdered sugar, beating until soft peaks form. Cover and chill until ready to serve.

  Drizzle each serving of pie with 1 tablespoon praline liqueur. Top with whipped cream mixture. Yield: 6 servings.

*For pecan pie, we used Edwards.

Piecrust Pointers

For the crumb crust pies in this chapter, we call for commercial crumb crusts. They're available in two sizes, 9 ounce and 6 ounce — and that's how they're labeled in the store. Each holds a different amount of filling, so it's important to use the correct size.

•For a 9-inch pie, we call for a 9-ounce commercial graham cracker crust (extra serving size). The 9-ounce crust has a banner on the label that reads "2 extra servings." This crust is not unusually large; it's actually the same size as a homemade crumb crust in a standard 9-inch pieplate.

•Sometimes we call for the smaller 6-ounce commercial graham cracker crust. The 6-ounce crust is much smaller than a standard 9-inch pieplate. If you use the 6-ounce crust in a recipe calling for a 9-inch or 9-ounce crust, the filling won't all fit.

•You'll also find shortbread crusts, chocolate crusts, and reduced-fat crusts available in the same sizes.

Peanut Butter Cream Pie

PREP: 12 MINUTES   CHILL: 8 HOURS

1 (8-ounce) package cream cheese, softened
1 cup sifted powdered sugar
1 cup chunky peanut butter
½ cup milk
1 (8-ounce) container frozen whipped topping, thawed

1 (9-ounce) commercial graham cracker crust (extra serving size) or chocolate graham cracker crust
¼ cup coarsely chopped peanuts

•Soften cream cheese for this pie by removing the foil wrapper and placing cheese on a microwave-safe plate or wax paper. Microwave at MEDIUM (50% power) one minute.

Combine first 4 ingredients; beat at medium speed of an electric mixer until blended. Fold in whipped topping; spoon into crust, and sprinkle with peanuts. Cover and chill 8 hours. Yield: 8 servings.

NO-BAKE CHOCOLATE
CHIP COOKIE PIE

No-Bake Chocolate Chip Cookie Pie

PREP: 7 MINUTES   CHILL: 8 HOURS

•Milk and cookies make this pie. Dunk chocolate chippers in milk, and layer them in the crust with whipped topping. As the pie chills, the moist layers become a yummy filling.

1 (15- or 18-ounce) package chocolate chip cookies*
1 cup milk
1 (9-ounce) commercial graham cracker crust (extra serving size)

1 (8-ounce) container frozen whipped topping, thawed

Dip 8 cookies in milk, and place in a single layer in graham cracker crust. Top with one-third of whipped topping. Dip 8 more cookies in milk, and place on top; spread with one-third of whipped topping. Repeat layers with 8 more cookies, milk, and remaining whipped topping. Crumble 2 chocolate chip cookies, and sprinkle over pie. Cover and chill 8 hours before serving. Yield: 8 servings.

*For cookies, we used Nabisco Chunky Chips Ahoy. You'll need 26 cookies for this recipe (you may have a few leftover cookies in the package).

Caramel Pie

PREP: 10 MINUTES   COOK: 1 HOUR AND 20 MINUTES
CHILL: 2 HOURS

2 (14-ounce) cans sweetened
    condensed milk
1 (6-ounce) commercial
    graham cracker crust
2 cups frozen whipped
    topping, thawed

1 (1.4-ounce) English toffee-
    flavored candy bar,
    chopped

Pour condensed milk into an 11- x 7- x 1½-inch baking dish; cover with aluminum foil. Place in a 13- x 9- x 2-inch baking dish; add hot water to larger dish to depth of 1-inch. Bake at 425° for 1 hour and 20 minutes or until condensed milk is thick and caramel colored (add hot water to larger dish as needed). Remove smaller dish from larger dish. Pour caramelized milk into crust; let cool.

Spread whipped topping over caramel filling, and sprinkle with chopped candy bar. Cover and chill at least 2 hours. Yield: 6 servings.

Variations:

For **Banana Caramel Pie,** slice 2 bananas, and layer slices in crust before adding caramel filling.

For **Caramel-Fudge Pie,** spoon ⅓ cup hot fudge topping into crust; then add caramel filling, whipped topping, and candy.

For **Chocolate-Caramel Pie,** substitute 1 (6-ounce) commercial chocolate crumb crust for graham cracker crust.

- This is an indescribably luscious pie. You won't believe such a simple procedure could produce such flavor—until you taste it.
- You can leave the pie unattended while it bakes. And it's a great make-ahead candidate; bake and chill it a day ahead.

Frozen Lemonade Pie

PREP: 5 MINUTES
FREEZE: SEVERAL HOURS UNTIL FIRM

1 (14-ounce) can sweetened
    condensed milk
1 (6-ounce) can frozen
    lemonade concentrate,
    thawed and undiluted

1 (8-ounce) container frozen
    whipped topping, thawed
2 (6-ounce) commercial
    graham cracker crusts
Garnish: lemon slices

Fold condensed milk and lemonade concentrate into whipped topping; spoon evenly into crusts. Cover and freeze pies until firm. Garnish, if desired, before serving. Yield: 12 servings (2 pies).

- This pie slices neatly straight from the freezer.
- For one deep-dish pie, use one 9-ounce commercial graham cracker crust (extra serving size) instead of two 6-ounce crusts.

Banana Split Pie

- This frozen pie slices best with a warm knife. Just run the blade under hot water, and wipe it dry.
- When you're shopping for this frozen pastry crust, be sure the package says deep-dish. Otherwise, it may be too shallow to hold the filling.
- As an option, you can use ½ (15-ounce) package refrigerated piecrusts. Just bake it in a 9-inch pieplate.

1 (9-inch) frozen deep-dish pastry shell
1 (8-ounce) package cream cheese, softened
1 cup sifted powdered sugar
½ cup crunchy peanut butter
½ cup chocolate syrup
2 cups frozen whipped topping, thawed
2 ripe bananas, mashed
Additional chocolate syrup
Maraschino cherries (optional)

Bake pastry shell according to package directions; let cool.

Beat cream cheese at medium speed of an electric mixer until fluffy. Add powdered sugar and peanut butter, beating until blended. Gradually add ½ cup chocolate syrup, beating well. Fold in whipped topping and mashed banana. Spoon filling into pastry shell. Cover and freeze pie 8 hours. Let stand at room temperature 20 minutes before serving. Drizzle each serving with additional chocolate syrup, and top with cherries, if desired. Yield: 8 servings.

Chocolate Chip-Almond Pie

- You can freeze this candy bar pie up to one week.

6 (1.45-ounce) milk chocolate bars with almonds, broken
17 large marshmallows
½ cup milk
1 cup whipping cream
½ cup semisweet chocolate mini-morsels
1 (2-ounce) package slivered almonds
1 (9-ounce) commercial graham cracker crust (extra serving size)
Sweetened whipped cream or frozen whipped topping, thawed (optional)

Combine first 3 ingredients in a heavy saucepan; cook over low heat until candy bars and marshmallows melt, stirring often. Remove from heat. Let cool.

Beat whipping cream at high speed of an electric mixer until stiff peaks form. Fold whipped cream, mini-morsels, and almonds into chocolate mixture. Spoon filling into crust. Cover; freeze until firm. Dollop with sweetened whipped cream, if desired, before serving. Yield: 8 servings.

Chocolate Ribbon Ice Cream Pie

PREP: 5 MINUTES   COOK: 7 MINUTES
FREEZE: SEVERAL HOURS UNTIL FIRM

2 cups miniature marshmallows
1 cup (6 ounces) semisweet chocolate morsels or mini-morsels
1 (5-ounce) can evaporated milk
1 (9-ounce) commercial graham cracker crust (extra serving size)
1 quart vanilla ice cream, slightly softened
¼ cup semisweet chocolate morsels or mini-morsels
¼ cup chopped pecans

•For **Mocha Ice Cream Pie,** substitute one quart coffee ice cream for vanilla.

•If you buy two pints of ice cream instead of a quart, the ice cream will soften quickly and make layering the pie a cinch.

Combine first 3 ingredients in a heavy saucepan. Cook over medium heat until marshmallows melt, stirring often. Remove from heat, and let cool.

  Spoon half of sauce into crust; top with half of ice cream. Repeat layers. Sprinkle with ¼ cup chocolate morsels and pecans. Cover and freeze until firm. Let stand at room temperature 15 minutes before serving. Yield: 8 servings.

Frozen Peanut Butter Pie

PREP: 15 MINUTES   FREEZE: 4 HOURS

1 quart vanilla ice cream, softened
1 cup frozen whipped topping, thawed
⅔ cup crunchy peanut butter
1 (9-ounce) commercial graham cracker crust (extra serving size)
Hot fudge topping or chocolate sauce (optional)

Combine first 3 ingredients in a large bowl; stir until blended. Spoon into crust. Cover and freeze 4 hours or until firm. Let stand 5 minutes before serving. Drizzle with fudge topping, if desired. Yield: 8 servings.

Frosty Pumpkin Pie

PREP: 15 MINUTES   FREEZE: 8 HOURS

• Here's a new no-bake idea for pumpkin pie. Blend pumpkin with ice cream, and freeze it.

1 cup canned mashed pumpkin
½ cup firmly packed brown sugar
1 teaspoon ground cinnamon
¼ teaspoon ground nutmeg
⅛ teaspoon salt
⅛ teaspoon ground cloves

1 quart vanilla ice cream, softened
1 (9-ounce) commercial graham cracker crust (extra serving size)
Garnish: sweetened whipped cream

Combine first 6 ingredients, stirring well. Fold in ice cream. Spoon into crust; cover and freeze 8 hours. Let stand at room temperature 10 minutes before serving; garnish, if desired. Yield: 8 servings.

Toffee Ice Cream Dessert

PREP: 15 MINUTES
FREEZE: SEVERAL HOURS UNTIL FIRM

• This is an ideal supper club dessert. You can make it ahead, it will serve a crowd, and the ingredients can't miss.

3 cups cream-filled chocolate sandwich cookie crumbs
2 tablespoons butter or margarine, melted
½ gallon vanilla ice cream, softened
1 (7.5-ounce) package almond brickle chips

Commercial fudge sauce, heated
Frozen whipped topping, thawed
Maraschino cherries (optional)

Combine cookie crumbs and butter, stirring with a fork. Press firmly into bottom of a lightly greased 13- x 9- x 2-inch baking dish. Bake at 350° for 5 minutes. Let cool.

Spread half of ice cream over crust; sprinkle with half of brickle chips. Repeat layers. Cover and freeze until firm. Cut into squares to serve. Top each serving with fudge sauce, a dollop of whipped topping, and, if desired, a cherry. Yield: 15 to 18 servings.

Apricot Tortoni

PREP: 11 MINUTES   FREEZE: 8 HOURS

12 vanilla wafer cookies
1 pint frozen vanilla yogurt,
    softened
1 (10-ounce) jar apricot
    preserves

1 teaspoon almond extract
¾ cup vanilla wafer crumbs
1 (2.25-ounce) package sliced
    almonds, toasted

Place paper baking cups in muffin pans. Place 1 cookie in each baking cup. Combine yogurt, apricot preserves, and almond extract, stirring well. Spoon yogurt mixture evenly into baking cups. Sprinkle with wafer crumbs and almonds. Cover and freeze 8 hours. Yield: 12 servings.

•Tortoni is an Italian frozen dessert, usually containing whipped cream and crumbled cookies. This frozen yogurt version features apricot preserves that provide a fruity sweetness.

•Since this recipe makes a dozen, you can serve a few at a time and keep the extras frozen for another occasion.

TOFFEE ICE CREAM DESSERT

CHOCOLATE
COOKIE
ICE CREAM

Chocolate Cookie Ice Cream

PREP: 8 MINUTES
FREEZE: SEVERAL HOURS UNTIL FIRM

•Make your own cookies 'n' cream ice cream with these three ingredients, which you probably have on hand.

1 (16-ounce) package cream-filled chocolate sandwich cookies, coarsely crumbled (42 cookies)

½ gallon vanilla ice cream, slightly softened
1 (8-ounce) container frozen whipped topping, thawed

Combine crumbled cookies and softened ice cream, stirring just until blended. Fold in whipped topping. Spoon mixture into a 13- x 9- x 2-inch pan or other large shallow container. Cover and freeze until firm. Scoop into serving bowls. Yield: about 13 cups.

Bananas Glacé

PREP: 4 MINUTES   COOK: 5 MINUTES

⅓ cup spiced or light rum
⅓ cup apricot preserves
2 tablespoons butter or
    margarine

2 large firm bananas
Vanilla ice cream

Combine first 3 ingredients in a large skillet; cook over medium heat until preserves and butter melt.

  Peel bananas, and cut in half lengthwise. Cut each half into 6 pieces; add to skillet. Cook over low heat until thoroughly heated, stirring occasionally. Serve warm banana mixture over ice cream. Yield: 4 servings.

•*Glacé* is a fancy term for glazed. Use any kind of rum to glaze these bananas, or for an alcohol-free version, try ¼ cup apple juice or pineapple juice.

Banana Split Waffles

PREP: 5 MINUTES

4 frozen waffles, toasted
2 cups vanilla ice cream
2 ripe bananas, sliced
1 (8-ounce) can pineapple
    tidbits or crushed
    pineapple, drained

Chocolate syrup or hot fudge
    topping

Place 1 toasted waffle on each of four dessert plates. Place a scoop of ice cream on each waffle. Top each serving with banana slices, pineapple, and chocolate syrup. Serve immediately. Yield: 4 servings.

•Waffles furnish a crispy base for this breakfast bread turned into dessert.

HOT APPLE SPICE SUNDAE

Hot Apple Spice Sundae

PREP: 2 MINUTES   COOK: 3 MINUTES

•Toast nuts in a dry skillet over medium heat two to three minutes, stirring often.

2 tablespoons butter or margarine
2 tablespoons brown sugar
½ teaspoon ground cinnamon
1 (21-ounce) can apple pie filling

⅓ cup or 1 (2.25-ounce) package chopped walnuts, toasted
Vanilla ice cream

Melt butter in a saucepan; stir in brown sugar, cinnamon, and pie filling. Bring to a boil; remove from heat, and stir in walnuts. Serve warm over ice cream. Yield: 6 servings.

Baked Spiced Fruit

PREP: 5 MINUTES   COOK: 32 MINUTES

1 (16-ounce) can apricot
   halves in light syrup,
   drained
1 (16-ounce) can pear halves,
   drained
1 (15¼-ounce) can peach
   halves, drained
1 (15¼-ounce) can pineapple
   chunks or tidbits,
   drained

1 cup orange juice
⅓ cup firmly packed brown
   sugar
1 tablespoon lemon juice
4 whole cloves
1 (3-inch) stick cinnamon
Dash of salt

•Here's an easy summer or winter dish. It's good hot or cold.

Cut apricot, pear, and peach halves in half; place, along with pineapple, in an 11- x 7- x 1½-inch baking dish.

Combine orange juice and remaining 5 ingredients in a saucepan; bring to a boil, reduce heat, and simmer 2 minutes. Pour over fruit. Bake, uncovered, at 350° for 30 minutes. Let cool slightly. Serve warm, or cover and chill 8 hours. Remove cloves and cinnamon stick before serving. Yield: 8 servings.

Cherry Crunch

PREP: 7 MINUTES   COOK: 6 MINUTES

¾ cup quick-cooking oats,
   uncooked
½ cup all-purpose flour
½ cup firmly packed brown
   sugar
½ teaspoon ground cinnamon

⅓ cup cold butter or
   margarine, cut into pieces
1 (21-ounce) can cherry pie
   filling
½ teaspoon almond extract
Vanilla ice cream

•Assemble this fruit cobbler early in the day, and pop it in the microwave after dinner; pour coffee while it's cooking.

Combine first 4 ingredients. Cut in butter with a pastry blender until mixture is crumbly.

Combine pie filling and almond extract in a greased 1-quart baking dish. Sprinkle with crumb mixture. Microwave, uncovered, at HIGH 6 minutes or until thoroughly heated. Top each serving with ice cream. Yield: 4 to 6 servings.

Cherry Parfaits

PREP: 20 MINUTES   COOK: 4 MINUTES

•You can make this recipe all in one dish. Just spoon half of ice cream into a deep one-quart serving dish; top with half of pie filling and crumb mixture. Repeat layers.

2 tablespoons butter or margarine
¼ cup chopped almonds
1 teaspoon ground cinnamon
8 commercial oatmeal cookies, crumbled

3 cups vanilla ice cream, softened
1 (21-ounce) can cherry pie filling

Melt butter in a skillet over low heat; add almonds and cinnamon. Cook 3 minutes, stirring often. Remove from heat; stir in crumbled cookies.

Layer ice cream, crumb mixture, and pie filling evenly into six parfait glasses or dessert dishes. Serve immediately. Yield: 6 servings.

CHERRY PARFAITS

Baked Pears à la Mode

PREP: 4 MINUTES   COOK: 30 MINUTES

2 (16-ounce) cans pear halves,
    drained
½ cup honey
¼ cup butter or margarine,
    melted

1 cup crumbled coconut
    macaroons or amaretti
    cookies
Vanilla ice cream

Arrange pear halves in an 11- x 7- x 1½-inch baking dish. Combine honey and butter; pour over pears. Bake, uncovered, at 350° for 20 minutes. Sprinkle crumbled cookies over pears; bake 10 more minutes. Serve warm with ice cream. Yield: 6 servings.

Strawberry Shortcake

PREP: 14 MINUTES   COOK: 20 MINUTES

4 cups sliced fresh or frozen
    strawberries, thawed
½ cup sugar
2 cups biscuit and baking mix
⅔ cup half-and-half
¼ cup butter or margarine,
    melted

2 tablespoons sugar
1 large egg, lightly beaten
1 tablespoon sugar
1 (8-ounce) container frozen
    whipped topping, thawed,
    or 1½ cups whipping
    cream, whipped

•If you're in the mood for peaches, substitute four cups sliced fresh peaches for the strawberries in this shortcake.

Combine strawberries and ½ cup sugar, stirring gently. Cover and chill at least 20 minutes.

Meanwhile, combine biscuit and baking mix and next 4 ingredients; beat at high speed of an electric mixer 30 seconds. Spoon batter into a greased 8-inch round cakepan; sprinkle with 1 tablespoon sugar. Bake at 425° for 15 to 20 minutes or until golden. Let cool in pan on a wire rack 10 minutes; remove from pan, and let cool completely on wire rack.

Split shortcake in half horizontally. Place bottom half, cut side up, on a serving plate. Spoon half each of strawberry mixture and whipped topping over shortcake. Top with remaining shortcake. Spoon remaining whipped topping and strawberry mixture on top. Yield: 8 servings.

Mocha Dream

PREP: 6 MINUTES

1 tablespoon instant coffee granules	½ cup chocolate syrup
1 tablespoon hot water	Frozen whipped topping, thawed (optional)
1 cup milk	Grated chocolate (optional)
1 pint vanilla ice cream, softened	

Combine coffee granules and hot water; stir until coffee granules dissolve. Combine coffee, milk, ice cream, and chocolate syrup in container of an electric blender; cover and process just until smooth, stopping once to scrape down sides. Top each serving with whipped topping and grated chocolate, if desired. Serve immediately. Yield: 3 cups.

Pineapple Milk Shakes

PREP: 5 MINUTES

•Add ¼ teaspoon coconut extract to make mock piña colada shakes (minus the rum).

3 cups vanilla ice cream	½ cup milk
1 (8-ounce) can crushed pineapple, undrained	

Combine all ingredients in container of an electric blender; cover and process just until blended, stopping once to scrape down sides. Serve immediately. Yield: 4 cups.

Peach-Banana Blossom

PREP: 7 MINUTES

•You may have to break apart the frozen peach slices to measure them. Freeze the sliced banana, too, for an ultimate thick shake.

•Use fresh peach slices for a slightly thinner shake.

1 ripe banana, sliced	½ cup frozen vanilla yogurt or ice cream
1 cup orange juice, chilled	
1 tablespoon honey	2½ cups frozen peach slices

Combine first 4 ingredients in container of an electric blender; cover and process just until smooth. Add peach slices, a few at a time, processing just until smooth after each addition. Serve immediately. Yield: 3 cups.

Raspberry Milk Shakes

PREP: 5 MINUTES

1 (10-ounce) package frozen
  raspberries in syrup,
  partially thawed

½ cup milk
1 quart vanilla ice cream,
  softened

Combine raspberries and milk in container of an electric blender; cover and process until smooth. Add ice cream, and process just until smooth. Serve immediately. Yield: 5 cups.

•This is one of the prettiest shakes around—blushing pink from a handful of berries. Try making it a second time with chocolate ice cream instead of vanilla.

Chocolate Malted

PREP: 5 MINUTES

3 cups vanilla ice cream
½ cup milk
⅓ cup chocolate syrup

2 tablespoons malt-flavored
  drink mix* (optional)

Combine first 3 ingredients in container of an electric blender; cover and process just until smooth, stopping once to scrape down sides. Stir in drink mix, if desired. Serve immediately. Yield: 3 cups.

.

*For drink mix, we used Ovaltine.

•For a minty shake, replace chocolate syrup with chocolate-mint syrup. And if you like really thick shakes, use four cups of ice cream.

RASPBERRY
MILK SHAKE

MOCHA
DREAM

PEACH-BANANA
BLOSSOM

Caramel Sauce

PREP: 2 MINUTES   COOK: 5 MINUTES

¾ cup butter or margarine   1 cup whipping cream
1½ cups firmly packed brown
    sugar

Combine butter and brown sugar in a heavy saucepan; cook over medium heat, stirring constantly, until sugar dissolves. Gradually add whipping cream; cook, stirring constantly, until mixture comes to a boil. Remove from heat, and let cool slightly. Serve warm over ice cream, gingerbread, or pound cake. Yield: 2½ cups.

Chocolate - Mint Sauce

PREP: 3 MINUTES   COOK: 5 MINUTES

•If you don't have pepper-mint extract, you can still get maximum mint flavor by using one cup semisweet chocolate mint morsels.

1 cup (6 ounces) semisweet   1 (5-ounce) can evaporated
    chocolate morsels   milk
⅔ cup light corn syrup   1 teaspoon peppermint extract

Combine chocolate morsels and corn syrup in a small heavy saucepan. Cook over low heat, stirring constantly, until morsels melt. Remove from heat; gradually stir in evaporated milk and peppermint extract. Serve warm or chilled. Yield: 1¾ cups.

Fudge Topping

PREP: 2 MINUTES   COOK: 7 MINUTES

•This dessert sauce becomes thick and fudgy after it chills.

½ cup butter or margarine   ⅔ cup whipping cream
2 (1-ounce) squares semisweet   1 tablespoon light corn syrup
    chocolate   1 teaspoon vanilla extract
⅔ cup sugar

Melt butter and chocolate in a heavy saucepan over low heat. Stir in sugar and remaining ingredients; cook 7 minutes or just until mixture begins to boil. Remove from heat. Let cool slightly.

  Serve topping warm, or cover and chill. (Topping will thicken as it chills.) Serve over ice cream or pound cake. Store in refrigerator. Yield: 2 cups.

BITTERSWEET
MOCHA SYRUP

Bittersweet Mocha Syrup

PREP: 2 MINUTES   COOK: 6 MINUTES

⅓ cup cocoa

⅓ cup firmly packed brown
   sugar

1 level tablespoon instant
   coffee granules

1 (5-ounce) can evaporated
   milk

⅔ cup light corn syrup

⅓ cup water

•Splash a spoonful of this
decadent dark sauce into
your coffee, or serve it over
pancakes or crispy waffles
for dessert.

Combine all ingredients in a saucepan. Bring to a rolling boil over
medium heat, stirring constantly; boil 2 minutes. Remove from heat;
let cool. Serve at room temperature over ice cream. Yield: 2 cups.

Index

Credits

**OXMOOR HOUSE WISHES TO THANK
THE FOLLOWING MERCHANTS:**

Augusta Glass Studio, Augusta, MO
Casafina, Brewster, NY
Cutco Cutlery, Olean, NY
Cyclamen Studio, Inc., Berkeley, CA
Eigen Arts, Inc., Jersey City, NJ
E & M Glass Ltd., Cheshire, UK
Fioriware, Zanesville, OH
Lamb's Ears Ltd., Birmingham, AL
Linden Mill Glass, Selkirkshire, UK
The Loom Company, Aletha Soulé, New York, NY
Luna Garcia, Venice, CA
Mariposa, Manchester, MA
Pastis and Company, New York, NY
Potluck Studios, Accord, NY
Carolyn Rice Art Pottery, Marietta, GA
Jill Rosenwald Ceramic Design, Boston, MA
Sabre Flatware, New York, NY
Smyers Glass, Benicia, CA
Two's Company, Mount Vernon, NY
Vietri, Hillsborough, NC

Contributing Photographers:
Ralph Anderson
Tina Cornett

Metric Equivalents

The recipes that appear in this cookbook use the standard United States method for measuring liquid and dry or solid ingredients (teaspoons, tablespoons, and cups). The information in the following charts is provided to help cooks outside the U.S. successfully use these recipes. All equivalents are approximate.

Metric Equivalents for Different Types of Ingredients

A standard cup measure of a dry or solid ingredient will vary in weight depending on the type of ingredient. A standard cup of liquid is the same volume for any type of liquid. Use the following chart when converting standard cup measures to grams (weight) or milliliters (volume).

Standard Cup	Fine Powder (ex. flour)	Grain (ex. rice)	Granular (ex. sugar)	Liquid Solids (ex. butter)	Liquid (ex. milk)
1	140 g	150 g	190 g	200 g	240 ml
¾	105 g	113 g	143 g	150 g	180 ml
⅔	93 g	100 g	125 g	133 g	160 ml
½	70 g	75 g	95 g	100 g	120 ml
⅓	47 g	50 g	63 g	67 g	80 ml
¼	35 g	38 g	48 g	50 g	60 ml
⅛	18 g	19 g	24 g	25 g	30 ml

Useful Equivalents for Liquid Ingredients by Volume

¼ tsp						=	1 ml		
½ tsp						=	2 ml		
1 tsp						=	5 ml		
3 tsp	=	1 tbls			=	½ fl oz	=	15 ml	
		2 tbls	=	⅛ cup	=	1 fl oz	=	30 ml	
		4 tbls	=	¼ cup	=	2 fl oz	=	60 ml	
		5⅓ tbls	=	⅓ cup	=	3 fl oz	=	80 ml	
		8 tbls	=	½ cup	=	4 fl oz	=	120 ml	
		10⅔ tbls	=	⅔ cup	=	5 fl oz	=	160 ml	
		12 tbls	=	¾ cup	=	6 fl oz	=	180 ml	
		16 tbls	=	1 cup	=	8 fl oz	=	240 ml	
		1 pt	=	2 cups	=	16 fl oz	=	480 ml	
		1 qt	=	4 cups	=	32 fl oz	=	960 ml	
						33 fl oz	=	1000 ml	= 1 l

Useful Equivalents for Dry Ingredients by Weight

(To convert ounces to grams, multiply the number of ounces by 30.)

1 oz	=	1/16 lb	=	30 g
4 oz	=	¼ lb	=	120 g
8 oz	=	½ lb	=	240 g
12 oz	=	¾ lb	=	360 g
16 oz	=	1 lb	=	480 g

Useful Equivalents for Length

(To convert inches to centimeters, multiply the number of inches by 2.5.)

1 in				=	2.5 cm			
6 in	=	½ ft		=	15 cm			
12 in	=	1 ft		=	30 cm			
36 in	=	3 ft	=	1 yd	=	90 cm		
40 in				=	100 cm	=	1 m	

Useful Equivalents for Cooking/Oven Temperatures

	Fahrenheit	Celcius	Gas Mark
Freeze Water	32° F	0° C	
Room Temperature	68° F	20° C	
Boil Water	212° F	100° C	
Bake	325° F	160° C	3
	350° F	180° C	4
	375° F	190° C	5
	400° F	200° C	6
	425° F	220° C	7
	450° F	230° C	8
Broil			Grill